Shut the F*ck Up, Listen and Be Heard

The No-Bullshit Guide to Real Connection

Kelsey Pearce

AI: The embedded images were created using napkin.ai, a tool that takes provided information and converts it into an information diagram.

Table of Contents

Preface

I've been a f*cking great listener my whole life. I don't say that to brag — I say it because, from as early as I can remember, it was my default role.

In grade school, while other kids were playing tag or trying to trade pudding cups, I was basically running a therapy session every recess. Kids would take turns sharing their squabbles, eight-year-old heartbreaks, and schoolyard drama, and I would listen. Patient. Calm. Trustworthy. Even a few of the moms knew they could sit with me and unload their frustrations, as if I were some miniature Dr Phil in sneakers.

Listening has always been my superpower; listening and sarcasm, to be more specific. I have the mug to prove it. But here's the catch: I've always been terrible at being heard. Somewhere along the way, my voice got lost in the noise of everyone else's. Maybe that's why sarcasm and wit became my default speaking style — if I couldn't hold someone's attention with honesty, I'd at least get a laugh. That's the dark little trade-off of being the one who listens: you risk becoming invisible.

This book was born out of that tension — the tug-of-war between listening and being heard. Because listening isn't passive, and it sure as hell isn't about being invisible. It's about connection. And when done right, it makes your words matter more when it's finally your turn to speak.

So yes, this is a book about listening. But it's also a book about being heard. It's for everyone who ever poured their heart out to the "schoolyard therapist" and never learned how to return the favour. It's for the partners, leaders, friends, parents, and coworkers who think they're listening but aren't. And it's for anyone who's ready to shut the f*ck up, lean in, and finally master the art of connection.

If you've read any of my other work, you might notice a shift in voice. My earlier books carried a softer tone — calm, mindful, filled with gratitude and reflection. This book is different. This one's a shake-up. Edgier. More raw. Less "find your centre" and more "get your sh*t together."

I've realized something in writing this book: maybe I stumbled into a writing career because it gave me the one thing I never had as a listener — the chance to finally be heard. So, thank you for listening.

Part I

The Noise We Swim In

We live in a world where everything is loud: family dinners that sound like debate clubs, Twitter threads that feel like brawls, meetings where the loudest voice wins. This section is about diagnosing the epidemic of noise — why we talk more than we listen, what it costs us, and how we can take listening seriously again. Think of it as the MRI scan before treatment: we're zooming in on what's broken.

Introduction

We are drowning in noise.

Scroll through Twitter (or X, or whatever we're calling it this week), and you'll see thousands of people convinced they're right, blasting hot takes into the void. Nobody's listening; everyone's waiting for their turn to dunk. Watch a political debate — it's not a dialogue, it's two trains colliding. And don't even get me started on meetings. You know the ones: thirty minutes of "collaboration" where nothing gets decided, except who can interrupt the most and still look like a team player.

And then there's home. Family dinners, car rides, date nights. Half the time we're not listening to each other — we're composing mental drafts of what we're going to say the second there's a pause. It's less conversation, more competitive storytelling.

I have lain in bed mentally drafting my side of a future conversation, or even worse, rehashing old conversations, trying to influence the outcome.

Here's the uncomfortable truth: most of us are not bad people; we're just bad listeners.

Why Listening Matters More Than Ever

The cost of poor listening is everywhere. Leaders fail because they bulldoze over their teams. Couples collapse because one partner feels invisible. Parents miss what their kids are really saying because they're too busy rehearsing a lecture. Every day, problems get bigger not because we don't talk enough, but because we don't listen enough.

And science backs this up. Research shows that when we feel truly listened to, our stress decreases, our trust increases, and we're more likely to cooperate. On the flip side, when we feel ignored, our brains literally register it as pain. That's right: being dismissed in conversation can hurt as much as stubbing your toe. Unlike a stubbed toe, the pain of being ignored may not heal or may take a long time to heal.

We live in a world where the boisterous voice is often the most rewarded, even now. Regardless of the lies and senseless filler it may contain, it is undeniably sensational and entertaining.

Listening Isn't Passive

Part of the reason listening feels undervalued is that people mistake it for being quiet. They think it's passive. Weak. Submissive.

Wrong. Listening is active. It takes attention, curiosity, patience, and sometimes restraint. It's about absorbing information, tracking subtext, and understanding emotion — all while resisting the urge to make it about you. It's a skill. A strategy. And when done well, it's a superpower.

Think about the people who command respect in your life. Odds are, they're not the ones who shout the loudest. They're the ones who make you feel heard. That's not an accident — that's listening as influence.

What You'll Find in This Book

This book is divided into five parts, and each one builds toward making you a better listener *and* more powerfully heard:

Part I — The Noise We Swim In

Why we're terrible at listening right now—and why it matters.

- **Introduction**
- **Chapter 1: The Epidemic of Noise**

Part II — The Core Skills of Listening

What real listening is (and isn't): stay engaged, validate, ask better questions, don't hijack.

- **Chapter 2: What Listening Really Is (And Isn't)**
- **Chapter 3: How to Listen Without Losing Yourself**
- **Chapter 4: Verbal Responses That Keep You in Listening Mode**

Part III — From Listening to Being Heard

How listening earns you credibility—and how to speak so people actually listen back.

- **Chapter 5: When You Really Have Something to Say**
- **Chapter 6: Getting Others to Listen to You**

Part IV — Contexts & Dynamics

How listening changes in one-on-one conversations, in groups, and without visual cues.

- **Chapter 7: Listening In-Person (One-on-One)**
- **Chapter 8: Listening in Groups & Teams**

Part V — Pressure-Tested & Practiced

High-stakes conversations, inner listening, labs, and real-world case studies.

Why This Book Will Be Different

There are numerous books on communication. Some are too clinical. Some are too soft. This one is neither.

This book will tell you the truth: you're not as good a listener as you think you are. It will also give you the tools — and the occasional kick in the ass — to change that. Along the way, we'll laugh at ourselves, learn from research, and practice the kind of listening that transforms relationships, careers, and communities.

So here's my ask: read this book with the same focus you'd want from someone listening to you. No multitasking. No mental drafting of your next point. Just lean in and take it in.

Because in a world addicted to noise, the most radical thing you can do is shut the f*ck up — and listen.

Chapter 1

The Epidemic of Noise

We live in a world where even our refrigerators want to talk to us. No, really — mine has Wi-Fi. Not only does it jingle if the door is left open, but it will also send a message to my cell phone. It also reminds me I haven't been using all the ice features, such as the craft ice, which hasn't been used in the last five days. Do I even open the message? No, it's a perfect metaphor for modern life: everything is talking, nobody is listening. At this point, I have ignored my GPS navigation enough that I expect it to give me false directions or a snarky attitude.

The Family Dinner Disaster

Picture this: a big family dinner. At one end of the table, Aunt Carol is going off about politics. Across from her, your teenage cousin is FaceTiming his girlfriend, who is also talking over Carol. Your dad is monologuing about his golf swing, complete with a salt-shaker-as-driver demo, while your mom is trying to tell a story that nobody is catching because Uncle Bill just started a rant about gas prices. Meanwhile, you're mid-sentence, trying to share some good news from work — and not a single pair of ears is on you.

It's chaos. It's exhausting. And it's not just family dinners. This is our culture. We've become masters at making noise and amateurs at making meaning.

The Science of Why We Talk Too Much

It's not entirely our fault. Neuroscience shows that talking about ourselves actually lights up the brain's reward centres. The same hit you get from food or sex, you get from talking about how your boss is an idiot or your dog is cuter than everyone else's. Harvard research found that people are willing to give up money to talk about themselves. Think about that: they'd rather be broke than be silent.[1]

Add social media to the mix, and it's no wonder our attention spans have tanked. A Microsoft study[2] reported that the average human attention span has shrunk to eight seconds — shorter than a goldfish's. That means by the time you finish saying, "I need to tell you something important," half the people in earshot are already mentally swiping through TikTok videos in their head.

The Chronic Interrupter Test

Score yourself today:

- Do people sigh before you finish a story?
- Do people say, "Let me finish..." multiple times?

---

[1] **Tamir, D. I., & Mitchell, J. P. (2012).** *Disclosing information about the self is intrinsically rewarding.* Proceedings of the National Academy of Sciences, 109(21), 8038–8043.

[2] **Microsoft Canada (2015).** *Attention Spans: Consumer Insights Report.*

- Do your texts look more like press releases than conversations?

If you answered yes to two or more, you're not just part of the noise—you might be its DJ. Time to recalibrate.

Cultural Comedy and Tragedy of Noise

If you want a crash course in how bad we've got at listening, watch a political debate. It's less about policies and more about who can shout louder, cut off more opponents, and land a zinger before the timer buzzes. It's tragic, sure, but also comedy gold. You can practically hear the world collectively groaning: "For the love of cheese, will someone just answer the damn question?"

Think back to the first Trump–Biden debate in 2020. It looked more like a brawl than a discussion. Trump repeatedly interrupted, jeered, and bulldozed Biden—even moderator Chris Wallace had to plead, "Please follow the rules."[3]

It wasn't substance that ruled—it was the shouting. That kind of chaos mirrors your family dinners when everyone talks over each other. Debates should be about clarity, not noise—and neither should your DMs or your Zoom rooms.

Sitcom Chaos vs. Real Life

Reflect on your favourite sitcoms. Friends, Seinfeld, The Office—half their punchlines rely on miscommunication,

---

[3] Anne Gearan, Philip Rucker, and Annie Linskey, "Trump incessantly interrupts and insults Biden as they spar in acrimonious first debate," *The Washington Post*, September 30, 202

interruptions, or people simply not listening. The comedy is **fuelled** by chaos.

Take Friends. Picture Monica's apartment: Chandler cracking a joke, Phoebe going off on a tangent, Joey shouting about food, Ross over-explaining dinosaurs, and Rachel trying to get a word in. It's chaos. It's hilarious—because you, the viewer, are safely outside the noise, watching it spiral.

Here's the twist: in real life, nobody is rolling credits after 22 minutes. That same chaos—everyone talking, nobody listening— isn't funny when it's happening at your weekly staff meeting, your family dinner, or in a group chat where your one important point gets buried under GIFs.

Sitcoms show us what happens when people don't listen: confusion, conflict, hijinks. It works on TV because misunderstandings can be solved in 30 minutes. In your workplace? Miscommunication costs money. In your family? It costs trust.

The laugh track covers the pain in sitcoms. Real life doesn't give you a laugh track.

Why This Matters

This constant noise comes with a price tag. Poor listening erodes relationships; partners feel dismissed, kids feel unseen, and employees feel invisible. It undermines leadership. It fuels conflict. And it's one of the main reasons we spend more time circling the same arguments than actually solving problems.

The truth? We're bad at listening because we've been taught that being heard is the prize. But here's the paradox: when nobody listens, nobody's really heard.

Quick Self-Check: Are You a Chronic Interrupter?

Let's test your noise levels. Answer yes or no to the following:

1. While someone else is talking, do you find yourself planning what *you* want to say next?
2. Do you ever interrupt someone mid-story to share your own?
3. Have you nodded along in a conversation and then realized you didn't catch half of what was said?
4. Do you finish people's sentences "for them"?
5. Do you ever think, "Hurry up and get to the point," while someone's speaking?

If you answered "yes" to three or more, congratulations — you're part of the epidemic. Again, not your fault. This wasn't an "are you a narcissist" quiz; not that we are selfish or intending harm. We just haven't practiced being in the moment, actively listening. It is the difference between listening to speak versus listening to hear. All about how we focus.

***

The epidemic of noise is real, but it's not permanent. This book isn't about silencing yourself forever. It's about understanding the cost of noise, reclaiming the lost art of listening, and learning how to turn listening into your unfair advantage. Because in a world addicted to talking, the person who truly listens is the one who will always have the power.

Reflection Prompt

Quick jot → Count how many times you interrupted (or were interrupted) today.

Medium reflection → Which interruptions mattered? Which were just noise?

Deep journaling → Write about a conversation that felt like chaos. What could you have done to make space for real listening?

Part II

The Core Skills of Listening

Listening isn't magic — it's a skill. And like any skill, it can be sharpened. In this part, you'll learn the nuts and bolts of staying engaged, validating without hijacking, and interrupting without steamrolling. These are the mechanics of listening: what to say, what not to say, and how to keep your mind from wandering while someone is still talking. If Part I highlighted the problem, Part II provides you with the starter toolkit.

Chapter 2

What Listening Really Is (And Isn't)

Let me tell you about two very different "listeners."

The first is a therapist I once sat across from with my son. She leaned forward. She nodded like one of those bobblehead dolls. Every pause was filled with the same robotic line: "Yes, I see." Except she didn't. Because at one point, she repeated the one thing he had specifically asked her not to bring up. Boom! Trust shattered.

The second listener is the friend you call when you've had a day from hell. They don't give advice. They don't hijack your story with a "that happened to me too!" They just… listen. They make you feel like you're the only person in the world worth paying attention to in that moment. By the time you hang up, nothing about your external reality has changed — but somehow, you feel lighter.

That's the difference between pretend listening and active listening. One looks the part. The other actually connects.

Myth-Busting: Listening Is Not Just "Not Talking"

Most people think listening means shutting your mouth and letting the other person talk. Wrong. That's called *waiting for your turn.* And honestly, some of us aren't even that good at it.

Listening is not about perfect silence, polite nodding, or sprinkling in "uh-huh" at random intervals. True listening requires effort. It's focus. It's curiosity. It's empathy. And — spoiler alert — it's also a strategy.

If you've ever sat through a conversation where someone kept saying things like, "Yeah, totally, same" or "I know exactly how you feel" … you know what faux-listening feels like. It's like talking to a wall that occasionally burps back familiar noises. You don't feel heard — you feel placated.

The Science of Real Listening

Let's get a little nerdy for a second. When you're listening, your brain is doing two big jobs:

1. Attention: filtering out distractions and staying present. (This is harder than ever thanks to our attention spans now clocking in shorter than a goldfish's — thanks, Microsoft.)

2. Empathy: mapping the other person's emotional state using your mirror neurons. That's why you sometimes tear up when someone else cries, or wince when they describe stubbing their toe.

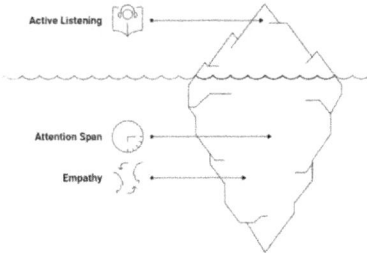

Real Listening Involves More Than Just Hearing

When someone feels deeply listened to, their stress hormones drop, trust rises, and they're more likely to open up. Carl Rogers[4], the psychologist who essentially put *active listening* on the map, said it best: it's about "entering the private perceptual world of the other and becoming thoroughly at home in it." In other words, it's not about standing outside their house; it's about stepping inside, sitting on their couch, and actually noticing the colour of the walls.

Cultural Role Models (and Trainwrecks)

If you want to see a listening masterclass, watch Oprah. She leans in. She waits. She pauses in just the right places so the guest fills the silence. Oprah validates without hijacking. She makes people feel seen, which is why they end up confessing things they didn't plan to say on national TV.

Now contrast that with certain late-night interviews where the host constantly interrupts to deliver a punchline. You know the kind: the guest is mid-story about something vulnerable, and suddenly it's derailed with a joke about pizza rolls. The audience laughs, but the guest? They retreat. Connection lost.

---

[4] **Rogers, C. R. (1957).** *The necessary and sufficient conditions of therapeutic personality change.* Journal of Consulting Psychology, 21(2), 95–103.

One approach builds trust. The other kills it.

When You Don't Have to Listen Like a Saint

The listening we are aiming for is not passive; it is active. Activity uses energy; therefore, active listening can be bloody exhausting. We cannot spend the entire day on a treadmill without collapsing; likewise, we cannot be engaged in deep listening by default.

It is about contextual listening. When do you need to activate your inner Oprah, and when can you give her a break? The following are three examples where context allows us a little grace from engaged listening:

- **The Boring Zoom Call**: If someone's reading slides word-for-word while your camera is off, it's fine if your brain takes a field trip. You don't need to memorize every bullet point about Q3 revenue. Tune back in if they suddenly stop screen-sharing and say your name.

- **The Group Free-for-All**: When a conversation has already been hijacked three times, feel free to hijack it back if it means getting to an actual point. Sometimes fair play means fighting fire with fire.

- **The Aunty Mai Saga**: We all have one — the relative or colleague who tells the same story every Friday call, like clockwork. Active listening doesn't mean re-enacting *Groundhog Day*. Throw in a filler, "oh wow," or "that's something," and let her roll. You don't watch the same soap opera rerun five times, so don't feel guilty if you don't lean in like it's fresh material.

So when do you listen deeply?

Start with active listening by default, then make a judgment.

- If the topic is *important,* an organizational update on leaders, teams, and responsibilities at work. You will want to understand the impact on yourself and others. How will this change the project you have in the hopper? Is there something missing that you may need clarification on?

- If it's *complicated,* your book club has decided to shake things up. The next novel takes place in London, England, with complicated tube rides throughout the city. The club is discussing a trip to follow the path of the book. There will be a lot of details — the when, who, how…? There is going to be a lot of noise in the muddled conversation, but you need to pay attention to the nuggets that may determine what is important to you for this adventure.

- If it's *revealing,* Aunty Mai drops a bombshell about the romantic comings and goings of Blue Skies Retirement Village. This may be interesting, or Aunty Mai might be in the middle of a love triangle and need emotional support.

Active listening is like a spotlight. You don't need it blazing all the time — just when the moment deserves it.

The Zoom Video Rule

If you get lost on a client or team Zoom calls:

Either turn your camera on or threaten yourself to turn it on. Seeing and being seen keeps your brain anchored in the moment. The threat of others seeing you are still in your PJs can be equally motivating.

If you find yourself zoning out, it's okay to turn off your camera—but only when there's no real work happening.

This gives you flexibility without taking you completely off the radar.

The Listening Spectrum

So if listening isn't just "being quiet," what is it? Think of it as a spectrum. You don't always need to be at the far end — sometimes it's perfectly fine to hover in the middle or even zone out for a bit. The actual skill is knowing *when* to shift gears.

Picture this: It's your cousin's birthday potluck. Half the family is crammed into the kitchen, the kids are running wild, and Aunt Mai is already warming up her retirement village soap opera saga. Here's how the spectrum plays out:

1. **Passive Listening**

   - You're hearing words, but not really engaging.

   - At the potluck, Uncle Joe is on his third retelling of how he "almost went pro" in high school basketball. You nod, refill your plate, and mentally plan your escape route.

   - When to Leverage: harmless small talk, background chatter, or repeat stories you could mouth along with.

2. **Active Listening**

   - You're paying attention, showing interest, asking clarifying questions.

   - At the potluck, your cousin's giving directions for the group photo, and everyone's chaos erupts. You actually tune in and repeat back: "Got it, meet at the porch in five, wear the blue top."

- When to Leverage: situations that need clarity, details, or basic cooperation.

3. **Empathic Listening**

- You're tuning into emotions, subtext, and what's not being said.

- At the potluck, your niece quietly admits she hates her new school while everyone else is laughing over cake. You catch the tone, put down your fork, and check in: "Hey, want to talk about that?"

- When to Leverage: when someone's feelings are on the line, or when subtle cues signal there's more going on beneath the surface.

4. **Strategic Listening**

- You're combining empathic listening with intent — using what you hear to respond effectively, build trust, or solve a problem.

- At the potluck, your sister vents about being overwhelmed with caregiving duties. You listen fully, validate her frustration, and then say, "Let's figure out a way to rotate weekend visits so you're not alone in this."

- When to Leverage: big conversations that call for action, trust-building, or solutions.

Levels of Listening Engagement

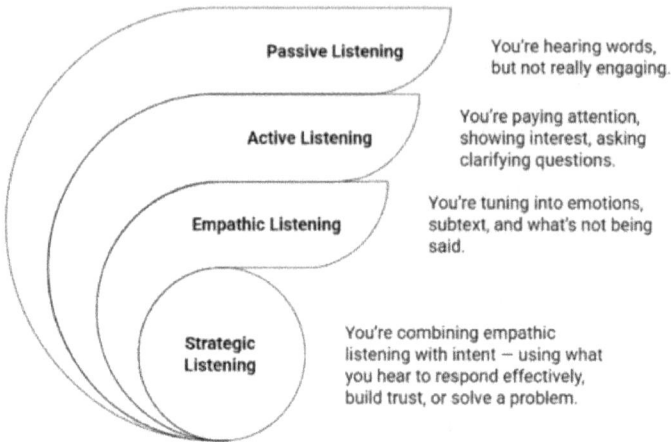

Passive Listening — You're hearing words, but not really engaging.

Active Listening — You're paying attention, showing interest, asking clarifying questions.

Empathic Listening — You're tuning into emotions, subtext, and what's not being said.

Strategic Listening — You're combining empathic listening with intent — using what you hear to respond effectively, build trust, or solve a problem.

The Listening Spectrum in Real Life

It's one thing to read "passive, active, empathic, strategic." It's another to see them in action. Here's how the spectrum actually plays out:

Passive Listening (Workplace): Your manager is explaining the new filing system. You nod politely, but in your head you're debating sushi vs. burrito for lunch. You'll probably need the email recap later.

Active Listening (Parenting): Your kid throws out, "I hate school." Instead of brushing it off, you lean in and ask, "What happened today?" Now you're engaging, not just hearing words.

Empathic Listening (Dating): Your date sighs, "I guess I'm just unlucky in love." The easy response is to cheerlead or give

16

advice. But empathic listening means you reflect the emotion: "That sounds lonely." Suddenly, they feel seen.

Strategic Listening (Business): In a negotiation, the other side hesitates when they mention the budget. You don't jump in immediately. You log it mentally — that's a pressure point, and knowing it lets you respond with precision.

You don't need to live at the "strategic" end of the spectrum 24/7 (which can be exhausting). But knowing which mode you're in — and when to shift gears — is what separates "kind of listening" from being a communication ninja.

Listening Norms Aren't Universal

Here's a curveball: everything I've just said about active, empathic, or strategic listening? It works — but not everywhere, not always, and not for everyone. Listening norms aren't universal.

Take silence. In the U.S., long pauses in conversation often make people squirm. We feel the need to fill the gap with "uh-huhs" and "so anyways." But in Japan, silence can be a mark of respect — it signals you're actually processing what's been said. What an American might label as "awkward," a Japanese colleague might consider "thoughtful."

Same with eye contact. In many Western cultures, "look me in the eye" is equated with honesty and engagement. But in parts of Asia or among Indigenous groups, prolonged eye contact can read as aggressive or disrespectful.

If you're thinking, "Great, so I'm doomed to offend everyone," take a breath. The point isn't to memorize a global etiquette manual. It's to approach listening with humility. Instead of assuming your interpretation of body language or silence is *the* interpretation, ask yourself: Could this mean something different here?

Erin Meyer, author of The Culture Map, puts it simply: communication is context. What feels natural in one culture can sound like nails on a chalkboard in another. Good listeners know when to adapt — and when to check their assumptions at the door.[5]

The Loudest Voice in the Room Might Be Your Own

Sitcoms like *Scrubs* or *Fleabag* nail this truth: we all have an internal narrator who never shuts up. J.D. in *Scrubs* will nod at a patient while internally daydreaming about a musical number. *Fleabag*'s asides to the camera show the mental chatter that constantly interrupts her actual conversations.

That's us every day. Even when we're not speaking, we're talking to ourselves. We're rehearsing our next line, remembering that awkward thing from last week, or silently crafting the perfect comeback.

Here's the problem: if your inner voice is hogging the mic, you can't fully hear anyone else. It's like trying to listen to a podcast while blasting another one in your earbuds.

---

[5] Meyer, E. (2014). *The Culture Map: Breaking Through the Invisible Boundaries of Global Business*. PublicAffairs.

So before we even talk about how to "actively listen" to others, we've got to admit this: sometimes the biggest interrupter isn't the loud guy at the dinner table. It's the voice in your own head.

We will review, giving your inner monologue centre stage in Chapter 11. To tame that inner monologue, we will review it in Chapter 12.

Practical Tool

Draw a quick spectrum line in your notes — **Passive** → **Active** → **Empathic** → **Strategic**.

Mark where you usually land, then ask: In which situations do I need to shift up (or down) the spectrum?

Remember: It's okay to sit at *Passive* sometimes. Not every conversation deserves your full Oprah-level attention. Save your energy for the moments that actually matter.

Zip Zone

Let's call out a few classic faux-listening hits:

- "Yeah, totally, same." (Translation: I wasn't actually listening, but I need to sound like I was.)

- "That reminds me of the time *I*…" (Ah, yes, the conversational hijacker strikes again.)

- "Don't worry about it; it's not that bad." (Dismissive, and also, thanks for invalidating my entire emotional experience.)

Are they wrong? We cannot determine without context and an assessment of your energy levels. Maybe the right response could have been, "Hey, this sounds really important to you, and I want to give you my full attention, but my energy is fully depleted. Can I call you in a few hours when I have recharged?" We will explore how to manage emotional vampires and protect your energy in the next chapter.

***

Listening isn't about silence. It's not about nodding politely. It's about being present, engaged, and tuned in at every level — from words to emotions and meaning. The best listeners don't just hear what's being said. They notice what isn't. They lean in.

But this superpower takes energy. It is not required in all situations.

> **Reflection Prompt:**
> Quick jot → Think of one conversation where you only "heard" but didn't "listen."
>
> Medium reflection → Which part of the spectrum (passive, active, empathic, strategic) do you default to?
>
> Deep journaling → Recall a sitcom-like "everyone talking over each other" moment in your life. How could it have played differently with real listening?

Chapter 3

How to Listen Without Losing Yourself

You've been there. A friend is ranting about a breakup — thirty minutes in, you've heard the story three different ways, and now you're nodding like a bobblehead doll on Red Bull. You aspire to be a good friend. You are a good friend. But when you finally hang up the phone (or stumble out of the coffee shop), you feel wrung out, like someone siphoned off your emotional energy and left you with lint.

You've just been drained by an emotional vampire.

The Trap of Over-Listening

Listening is powerful, but if you don't set boundaries, it can consume you. Being present doesn't mean becoming a sponge that soaks up everyone else's emotions until you're soggy. And yet, a lot of us fall into exactly that trap — we absorb the other person's feelings as if they were our own.

This doesn't make you empathetic. It makes you exhausted.

As psychologist Dr Judith Orloff, who has written extensively about *empaths* and energy drainers, puts it: "Empathy without boundaries is self-destruction." Orloff isn't anti-listening. She's pro-listening *with limits*.

Once you become the go-to listener, your role in a social group quietly shifts — and not always in your favour. You stop being seen as a whole person and start being slotted into a single identity: The Listener. That's what happened to me on the school grounds. I wasn't the classmate who played four-square or the friend who told jokes. I was the pseudo-therapist, the kid you sat with when you needed to unload your eight-year-old heartbreak. When people rely on you to absorb their stories, their drama, their emotions, they sometimes forget you have your own. You go from being part of the game to being in the bleachers. From participant to backdrop. And after a while, that can be crushing — because even the best listeners want, and deserve, to be heard.

Listener Trap Warning

Being a successful listener is a gift — but it comes with a catch.

Once you are known as The Listener, people treat you like a chair at a therapy session instead of a human with your own voice.

- You stop being invited into the game because you're expected to sit on the sidelines.
- Friends (or coworkers, or family) lean on you for support but forget to ask how you're doing.
- Your identity shrinks to "the person who listens," not "the person who also wants to be heard."

Also, here is the surprising part: when you are responsible for holding everyone's secrets, individuals may be more afraid of your memory than they are trusting of your presence. Instead of leaning in, they pull back — worried you've got a mental archive of all their mess.

Here's the truth: even the best listeners deserve airtime. Don't let your superpower turn you into background furniture — or a vault that others tiptoe around.

Flip-Side Note: The way out is balance — show that you're not just a vault, you're also a human. Share a little of yourself, even in small doses. When people see you talk and listen, they'll trust you without fearing you.

Friendship or Free Therapy?

Here's a hack: when you wonder if someone is a friend or just using you as free therapy, check for reciprocity. Do they ever ask how *you* are? Do they listen when you speak, or just wait until you stop breathing so they can jump back in?

A balanced relationship has an ebb and flow: sometimes you're the listener, sometimes you're the talker. But if the balance never tilts your way, you're being mined for emotional labour, not loved as a human being.

Soft exit scripts can help:

- "I really want to hear this, but I only have 15 minutes right now."

- "Can we pick this back up after dinner? My brain is fried."

- "I'm here, but I don't have the energy to problem-solve tonight. Can I just listen without giving advice?"

Boundaries don't make you cold. They make you sustainable.

The Neuroscience: "Name It to Tame It"

One of the most effective ways to stay present without being hijacked is a concept introduced by Dr Dan Siegel, a clinical professor of psychiatry at UCLA. He coined the phrase "name it to tame it."[6]

Here's how it works: when you listen to someone describe their emotions, and you reflect those feelings back with words — "It sounds like you're frustrated" or "You seem really disappointed" — it literally helps calm their nervous system. Brain imaging shows that labelling emotions reduces activity in the amygdala (the fight-or-flight centre) and increases activity in the prefrontal cortex (the rational thinking part).

In other words, you can be a lifeline for the speaker without drowning yourself in their emotional storm.

Tools for Protecting Yourself While Listening

Mental Note-Taking

Instead of just absorbing feelings, make quiet mental notes. Treat the conversation like you're the stenographer, not the co-star.

---

[6] Source: Siegel, D. J. (2012). *The Whole-Brain Child: 12 Revolutionary Strategies to Nurture Your Child's Developing Mind.* New York: Bantam Books.

Example: "Anger at boss. Feels overlooked. Wants recognition." This keeps your brain in observer mode rather than victim-by-proxy mode.

Breathing Anchor Exercises

When emotions run hot, ground yourself in your breath. A simple technique: inhale for four counts, hold for four, exhale for six. This slows your heart rate and keeps you calm, even if the other person is spiralling. Research from Harvard's Benson-Henry Institute for Mind Body Medicine shows that paced breathing triggers the relaxation response, countering stress.

The Emotional Coat Check

Visualize their emotions as a heavy coat. Imagine they hand it to you while they talk. Your job isn't to wear it around and sweat — it's to hang it in the coat check while you sit with them. When the conversation ends, you give it back. This little mental trick can be surprisingly powerful.

Spot Your Own Stress Before It Hijacks You

Listeners often pride themselves on absorbing emotions, but here's a twist: sometimes the emotional storm brewing is your own. Check yourself mid-conversation:

- Are your shoulders creeping up?
- Are you holding your breath?
- Are you rehearsing what you want to say instead of hearing them out?

These are your red flags. Catch them early, and you won't end up snapping, zoning out, or resenting the conversation. Self-listening is stress prevention.

The Reciprocity Rule: Real Friends Listen Back

Here's the blunt truth: if you are always the listener and never the speaker, that isn't a balanced friendship — it's a service arrangement. Free therapy. Emotional Uber. Call it what you want, but don't call it a connection.

Healthy relationships are reciprocal. Sometimes you're the shoulder to cry on, and sometimes you're the one crying. If that balance never happens — if you leave every interaction wrung out while the other person floats away lighter — you're not in a friendship. You're an emotional landfill. A dumping ground for freeloading clients.

So how do you reclaim balance without ghosting everyone who leans on you?

- Name the Pattern Out Loud: Try something as simple as, "I want to share something that's been on my mind too — can I take a turn?" Direct, clear, and hard to ignore.
- Set Small Boundaries: "I've got about 15 minutes to talk right now, but after that I need to switch gears." This caps the energy drain and signals you're not a 24/7 hotline.
- Ask for Reciprocity: "I'm glad you can trust me with this. Can I ask for the same in return?" Most real friends will rise to that cue.
- Make the Cut (When Needed): If someone consistently drains you, ignores your needs, and treats your listening like a utility

bill they don't have to pay, it may be time to downgrade their access to you. Not everyone earns VIP listener privileges.

Reality Check

If you're always "the strong one" in every relationship, check your circle. True friends don't just want your ears — they want your voice.

Zip Zone

Here's what listening isn't: offering unlimited, unpaid therapy. If you've ever thought, "I should charge hourly for this conversation," you're not alone. Listening is a gift, not a lifelong subscription.

Humour Meets Reality: The "Support Line" You Didn't Sign Up For

There's an old Seinfeld bit where Jerry talks about how friends basically become our "free therapists." And it's true. But unlike actual therapists, friends aren't trained to separate themselves emotionally, which is why listening can feel like carrying a backpack full of bricks that aren't yours.

This is where skill comes in. Real listeners know how to be present without paying for it with their sanity.

***

Listening without losing yourself is about striking a balance. You want to be engaged, compassionate, and present — but not a dumping ground for every passing emotion. Use the Siegel's name it to tame it trick. Anchor yourself with your breath. Take notes like an

27

observer. And for the love of your mental health, remember the coat check.

Because the best listeners aren't martyrs. They're steady, grounded, and still standing when the conversation ends.

Reflection Prompt:
Quick jot → Who in your life drains you most in conversation? Write their initials.

Medium reflection → How does your body react (tight chest, shallow breath, fidgeting) when you're being "emotionally dumped on"?

Deep journaling → Write a script for setting a boundary in that relationship. How can you maintain compassion without becoming an emotional wasteland?

Chapter 4

Verbal Responses That Keep You in Listening Mode

Picture this: Your friend says, "Work has been brutal lately, I feel like my boss is out to get me."

- **Option A (The Listener):** "That sounds rough. Tell me more—what's been happening?"

- **Option B (The Hijacker):** "OMG, my boss is the same way! One time she made me redo an entire report…"

Which one immediately conjured an image of the friend or acquaintance who always makes it all about them? I bet option B had you cringing at the image of the conversation hijacker. If you thought of yourself as the hijacker, great, you self-identified, and that is the first step to improvement.

The Problem with Words That Aren't Listening

Most of us think listening is just about not talking too much. But the few words you say can either:

1. Open the door wider: encouraging more trust, more depth, more connection.

2. Slam it shut: signalling, "Thanks for warming up the stage, now here's my performance."

Verbal responses are where listening either survives or dies.

The Science: Why Validation Works

Harvard Business School ran a series of studies on conversational satisfaction and found something shocking: it's not the length of time people talk that matters most, but whether they feel validated in the exchange.[7] When listeners use responses like "That makes sense" or "I can see why you'd feel that way", speakers report higher satisfaction—even if the conversation itself was short.

Translation: you don't have to be brilliant, you just have to prove you were paying attention. And if your goal is to impress, guess what? Listening is the flex.

Practical Tools

10 Listening Mode Templates

Use these as scaffolding until they become second nature:

1. "That sounds important—can you tell me more?"

2. "What was the hardest part of that for you?"

3. "How did you handle it?"

4. "That must've been [emotion word]."

5. "What do you need most right now?"

- [7] **Harvard Business School (2017).** *Research Spotlight: Why "Tell me more" is the best thing you can say in conversation.* Harvard Business Review.

6. "What do you think it means for you?"

7. "That's a lot—how are you feeling about it now?"

8. "What's the part that sticks with you the most?"

9. "How would you like it to go differently next time?"

10. "Tell me more about that." (Yes, this boring brief sentence is an MVP. Repeat it like it's your favourite playlist.)

4 Curious Language Templates

Instead of trying to build a connection with a 'me too' story, lean on curiosity. Swap in phrases like:

1. "I'm curious about..."

2. "What surprised you most?"

3. "How did you know it was time to...?"

4. "When you look back, what stands out most?"

Think of it as verbal scaffolding: you're helping them build their own narrative higher and stronger without grabbing the hammer out of their hands.

Zip Zone: What NOT to Say

Now for the fun part. Here's a hall of fame for responses that sound like listening but aren't. If you recognize yourself here, don't panic—we all do this. The key is being aware and leveraging more impactful responses when the context requires.

- "Anyway, did I tell you about my cat's gluten allergy?"

- "Same thing happened to me, only worse..."

- "You think *that's* stressful? Wait until you hear—"

- "Here's what you should do..."

- "At least it's not as bad as..."

- "Wow. Wild. Anyway..."

- "My cousin's roommate's uncle had that exact problem..."

- "That reminds me of a YouTuber..."

Each of these is basically conversational theft. Funny? Sometimes. Helpful? Never.

***

The words you choose don't need to be profound. They need to be positioning tools—a way of sliding the spotlight back onto the speaker instead of grabbing it for yourself.

If listening is a dance, your verbal responses are the gentle nudges that keep your partner twirling gracefully—instead of crashing into the wall.

Reflection Prompt:

Quick jot → Write three "curious" responses you can use tomorrow instead of hijacking.

Medium reflection → Replay a recent chat in your head. Where did you shift the spotlight to yourself instead of validating?

Deep journaling → Journal about the last time someone really validated you. What words did they use that stuck with you?

Part III

From Listening to Being Heard

Now we take these skills into the wild. Listening doesn't look the same across contexts — one-on-one with a friend, in a brainstorming session, on Zoom, or at a tense family dinner with Aunt Mai and her weekly soap opera recap. This section breaks down the dynamics of listening according to the setting. You'll learn how to read the room, track who's being ignored, and even navigate digital conversations where tone can get lost. Because if you can adapt your listening to the environment, you've already won half the battle.

Chapter 5

When You Really Have Something to Say

The Office Volcano

You're in a Monday morning meeting. The team is going in circles about why the sales deck isn't landing. You're sitting there, practically vibrating because you *know the answer.* You can see the slides in your head, you've already written a better hook, and if you don't say something soon, you're going to explode like a *Mentos* dropped in a bottle of *Coke.*

But you also know if you just blurt it out, you'll look like the office bulldozer—the guy who hijacks every brainstorm with *"Well, when I was at my last company…"* Cue the collective eye-roll.

So here's the tightrope: how do you cut in without cutting people down? How do you share your brilliant, world-saving point without being "that guy"?

The Myth of the Polite Listener

We're taught to wait our turn. But real life isn't kindergarten carpet time, and there's no magic talking stick that ensures everyone's wisdom gets heard. Sometimes the moment will *never* come unless you take it.

The catch? If you interrupt like a bulldozer, you lose trust. If you wait forever, you lose your voice.

That's where assertive, respectful interruption comes in. It's the art of saying: *"I hear you, I value what you're saying, but I also have something to add."* Think of it as conversational jiu-jitsu—you redirect the flow without breaking the rhythm.

The Psychology of Permission Language

Research in assertiveness training indicates that people respond more positively when interruptions are framed with *permission language.* Instead of barging in with *"Yeah, but…"*, you earn a sliver of space with phrases like:

- "Can I jump in for a second?"
- "Would it be okay if I added something here?"
- "May I offer a different angle?"

Why does this work? Because it softens the power move. According to clinical psychologist Manuel Smith (author of *When I Say No, I Feel Guilty*), assertiveness is not aggression—it's standing up for your perspective while respecting the other person's rights. Permission language tells the room: "I'm here, I'm confident, and I care about not steamrolling you."

And ironically, asking for permission often makes people *more* willing to listen to you. It's the verbal equivalent of knocking before you walk into someone's office instead of *Kool-Aid* Man-ing through the wall.

Helpful Hint: Tag-Team Interrupting

Confession: I suck at interrupting. One, it's not in my nature. Two, I've been a remote employee for over fifteen years, which means I've lost some of that "read the room" muscle when most of the team is in a physical conference room and I'm a face in a tiny Zoom square.

I once had a leader who valued my input and would make space by asking, "Kelsey, what's your perspective?" or "Does that make sense to you?" It wasn't official ally-ship, but it planted an idea: what if you collaborated with someone else who was also reserved and tag-teamed interruptions?

Here's how it works:

I interrupt not for myself, but to pull someone else in. Example: "Nadia, does that align with your perspective?"

Nadia does the same for me when I need space.

The beauty? You're not the bulldozer. You're the bridge. And you normalize the flow for quieter voices without hijacking the room.

Caveat: Don't overuse the tactic. If every third sentence is "Let's hear from so-and-so," it feels forced. But used sparingly, it's a respectful way to disrupt the noise and maintain a balanced conversation.

The Buddy System for Speaking Up

Sometimes the best way to interrupt is to let someone else do the heavy lifting with you. Try these hacks:

Tag-Team Interruptions: Pair with a colleague so you can cue each other in. Example: "I'd love to hear Nadia's take on this." It feels less self-promotional and spreads airtime.

Silent Signals: Agree on hand-raises, chat pings, or even a sticky-note on a camera (for remote calls) as a "my turn" cue. Low drama, high impact.

Role Rotation: For recurring meetings, suggest alternating facilitators. If the same people always dominate, rotating the chair forces airtime to be shared – and it develops leadership skills in quieter folks, too.

Anchor Ally: Before a meeting, ask one person to "call you in" if the flow is too fast. A simple, "I think Kelsey had a thought here," can reset the room.

These strategies don't just get you heard; they normalize space-sharing. The more you use them, the less it feels like "interrupting" and the more it feels like collaboration.

Practical Tools

The Permission Sandwich

Here's your new interruption toolkit. I call it the Permission Sandwich—three easy layers:

Acknowledge: show you've been listening.

- "I see the point you're making about timelines…"

Insert: Deliver your perspective concisely.

- "…but I think there's a faster way if we adjust the opening slide to highlight client pain points."

Hand Back: Return the floor.

- "Curious what you think about that tweak."

Boom. You're assertive, you're respectful, and you haven't turned into a conversational tank.

Scripts for Respectful Interruptions

Here's your ready-made script list. Steal liberally:

- "I want to make sure I'm understanding. May I jump in?"

- "Let me pause you for a second—I think I see a potential solution."

- "Can I add something that builds on what you just said?"

- "Sorry to cut in—I just want to flag one quick thought before we move on."

- "I think there's a point here that might save us time. Okay if I share?"

Notice the tone: polite, curious, framing yourself as additive, not combative.

Timing Tricks

Interrupting well isn't just *what* you say; it's about *when*.

- **Watch the Breath:** People naturally pause at the end of a thought. That's your golden ticket.

- **Use the Hand Cue:** Lean in slightly, raise a finger—not the aggressive pointer, just the *"hold that thought"* gesture. It signals you have something without words.

- **Stack the Deck:** Start with a validating nod or "Mm-hmm" so that when you speak, it feels like a continuation, not a derailment.

Zip Zone: Don't Be *That Person*

Let's play this out. Imagine you're in a brainstorming session and someone blurts:

- "Okay, enough about that. Here's what we're really doing…"

- "I don't care what anyone else thinks; here's my plan…"

- "Yeah, but you're wrong, so…"

They have just bulldozed the entire room. Everyone's trust? Gone. Their credibility? Torched.

Don't be that person. This person doesn't get invited to happy hour. That person gets muted on Zoom. They become a cautionary tale HR whispers about during onboarding.

Cultural Case Study: Permission in Action

Think about the best interviewers—Terry Gross, Oprah, Anderson Cooper. They interrupt *all the time.* But notice how? They do it with curiosity, validation, and brevity. It's never: *"Enough, now let's talk about me."* It's: *"Can I pause you there—when you said X, what did you mean?"*

It is a skill that requires practice.

***

The point isn't to stay silent until you combust. It's to learn how to cut in without cutting people off. Assertive interruptions, done right, make you the person everyone actually wants in the room: the one who moves things forward without leaving conversational carnage behind.

So next time you feel the need to word vomit all of your thoughts to a group of people, remember the Permission Sandwich. Acknowledge. Insert. Hand back.

And for the love of all things holy—don't be *that person.*

Reflection Prompt:
Quick jot → Practice writing one "permission phrase" ("Can I add something?").

Medium reflection → Recall a time you failed to interrupt and regretted it. How would you do it differently with ally or permission strategies?

Deep journaling → Write a plan for teaming with an "interrupt buddy." Who would you pick? How could you support each other in meetings?.

Chapter 6

Getting Others to Listen to You

The Invisible Voice

You know that colleague who stares at their phone when you talk, nodding like one of those dashboard bobbleheads? Or maybe it's your partner who zones out mid-story, only to ask you the exact question you literally just answered. You talk, they glaze. You explain again; they shrug. Somewhere deep inside you want to grab a megaphone, climb on the kitchen table, and scream: *"Can somebody just listen to me for once?!"*

Here's the truth: people don't automatically listen to you just because you're speaking. Presence isn't granted; it's earned. And ironically, the fastest way to earn it isn't by shouting louder; it's by listening better. Which is why this chapter serves as the pivot point — transitioning from listener-in-training to speaker-with-gravity.

Why People Tune You Out

We've all been guilty of zoning out. But when it happens to us repeatedly, it feels like slow erosion — like your voice is dissolving into the background noise. The culprit is usually one of three things:

Credibility Deficit

Why it happens: if people aren't sure you know your stuff, their brains file you under "ignore." (Like when your cousin Chad gives stock tips at Thanksgiving.)

How to fix it:

- Show your receipts. Drop a quick fact, stat, or lived experience that grounds your point: *"I've seen this in three product launches now — here's what worked and what tanked."*

- Start small, then scale. Share quick wins that build a track record. Credibility stacks like Lego — you don't need a castle right away, just a sturdy base.

Example: In a meeting about budget cuts, don't say, "I think we should…" Say: "Last quarter we trimmed X and saved $40k — here's where we can repeat the win."

Presence Problem

Why it happens: if you sound tentative, rushed, or apologetic, people mirror that by not taking you seriously. It's not about what you say, but how you land it.

How to fix it:

- Slow. The hell. Down. Nerves make us rush, but authority lives in pacing. Pauses create gravity.

- Drop the "sorry" tic. Stop apologizing for existing. Instead of "Sorry, I just wanted to add…" try "I'd like to add…" Small swap, big difference.

- Claim space physically. Even on Zoom, lean in slightly, raise your chin, and maintain eye contact with the camera.

Example: Think Steve Jobs on stage — he'd pause so long you wondered if he'd forgotten his lines. But no, he was milking silence until you leaned forward.

Noise Competition

Why it happens: In meetings, in relationships, in group chats — there's always something shinier, louder, or more dramatic fighting for airtime. If you're not intentional, you'll get drowned out.

How to fix it:

- Hook early. Lead with the line that matters, not a throat-clearing essay. ("Here's the 10-second version…")

- Use contrast. If everyone's shouting, go quieter. If everyone's vague, go crisp. Surprise is magnetic.

- Anchor with a story. Humans remember anecdotes way longer than bullet points.

Example: In a team brainstorm, instead of saying, "I kind of think we should revisit last quarter's campaign performance…" try: "Quick story: last quarter, one tweak in our ad copy doubled engagement. Let's do that again."

The Research: Why Listening Buys You Speaking Power

Amy Edmondson, the Harvard professor who coined the term *psychological safety*, found that when people feel heard, they're more willing to listen in return. It's reciprocal trust. You give space; they give it back. It's why the best leaders are also the best listeners — people don't just tolerate their voice; they lean in to hear it.

Neuroscience backs this up, too. When we feel validated, our brain's limbic system (emotional control centre) calms down, making us more receptive. Listening literally lowers defences, which means when it's your turn to talk, your audience isn't braced for attack — they're curious.

Cultural Example: The Steve Jobs Pause

Let's talk about Steve Jobs. Love him or hate him, the man knew how to hold a room. His secret weapon wasn't constant talking; it was silence. Jobs would ask a question or make a point, then *pause*. He let the room to breathe. He let people hang in the moment, waiting for his next word. That pause did two things:

1. Signalled confidence — he didn't rush to fill the space.

2. Made people hungry — silence-built tension, which gave his next word more weight.

You don't need a black turtleneck or a billion-dollar company to use the Jobs Pause. All you need is the courage not to word-vomit nervously the second you are given the floor.

The caveat to pausing is that if you don't own the stage, someone might want to fill that space. We have an aversion of quiet spaces. If you need a pause, you can always ask for it: "Hmm, let's pause on that thought for a few seconds."

Practical Tool: The "Hook, Bridge, Land" Framework

Want to sound credible and clear every time you speak? Use this three-step formula:

Hook—start with something that grabs attention. It can be a stat, a story, or even a simple "Here's what I noticed..." Don't bury your lead.

- Example: "In the last three months, customer complaints have doubled — but there's one simple fix."

Bridge—connect the hook to your principal message. This is where you link observation to insight.

- Example: "The issue isn't product quality; it's response time. We're slow, and people hate waiting."

Land—finish with clarity and impact. What do you want them to *do* with this information?

- Example: "If we cut reply times in half, complaints drop. I've got a three-step plan to make that happen."

This framework works everywhere: in meetings, arguments, even with your kids. Hook them, bridge the context, land your point.

Teen Example (a.k.a. The TikTok Attention Span Test):

If collectively we have a shorter attention span than a goldfish now, it is even worse for parenting a teenager or a wannabe teenager. It only takes a few seconds before they unpause the earbud tuning you want.

Hook—grab their attention before the eye-roll.

- "I noticed the car's gas light is on."

Bridge—connect the dots to something they actually care about.

- "If you run out of gas on the way to your friend's house, you're stuck — and I'm not bailing you out at midnight."

Land—deliver the takeaway with clarity (and maybe a little bite).

- "So fill it up today, or tomorrow you're Ubering on your own dime."

When the Power Balance Isn't Equal

Here's the thing about listening: it doesn't happen in a vacuum. Power messes with it. Put a manager in the room with an employee, a parent with a teenager, or a doctor with a patient, and suddenly the conversation is less about listening and more about who gets the final word.

If you've ever sat across from your boss and thought, "This is a performance, not a dialogue," you've felt it. If you've been a parent trying to pry more than a grunt out of your 15-year-old, you've felt it. And if you've ever sat in a doctor's office only to be cut off 11 seconds into describing your symptoms (yep, that's the research average), you've definitely felt it.

The problem? The person with more authority often assumes he / she / they're being heard simply because the other person is nodding along. Meanwhile, the person with less power is swallowing what they actually think because they don't feel safe enough to say it.

Amy Edmondson, the Harvard researcher who literally coined the term psychological safety, puts it bluntly: if people don't feel safe, they won't speak up. And when they don't speak up, mistakes happen, resentment festers, and listening collapses into compliance theatre.[8]

The Power Flip

So how do you fix it? Enter The Power Flip — a simple, intentional move that makes space for the quieter voice in the room. It works like this:

1. Name the Dynamic

Say the thing everyone's feeling, but no one wants to call out.

- "I know I'm your manager, but I want to hear your perspective before we move on."
- "I'm the parent, but I don't have all the answers. What's your take?"
- "I know I'm the doctor here, but you know your body better than I do. Tell me everything you've noticed."

2. Wait Longer Than Feels Comfortable

Silence is your friend here. Count to five if you have to. Research shows patients share far more accurate info when given uninterrupted time. (Doctors who resist the urge to jump in? Lower misdiagnosis rates.)[9]

---

[8] Edmondson, A. (1999). *Psychological safety and learning behavior in work teams.* Administrative Science Quarterly, 44(2), 350–383.

[9] Rhoades, D. R., McFarland, K. F., Finch, W. H., & Johnson, A. O. (2001). *Speaking and interruptions during primary care office visits.* Family Medicine, 33(7), 528–532.

3. Mirror, Then Add

Instead of steamrolling with your opinion, mirror what they said first.

- "So you're saying the deadlines feel unrealistic. Let's look at what's possible."
- "You're worried I don't trust you. I hear that. Here's where I'm coming from."

The goal isn't to flatten the power difference — it exists for a reason. The goal is to acknowledge it out loud so the other person doesn't feel invisible.

Example: The Doctor's Office

Two doctors, same patient.

- Doctor A: Cuts in after 11 seconds. Assumes the headache is "stress-related." Writes a prescription.
- Doctor B: Lets the patient finish describing symptoms. Turns out it's not stress at all — it's a rare side effect of medication. Correct diagnosis, faster recovery.

The difference wasn't brilliance. It was patience. It was listening.

Zip Zone: Don't Be the Spotlight Hog

Now, here's where people screw it up. They confuse "getting others to listen" with "hogging the mic." We've all been stuck in a meeting where someone drones on and on like they're auditioning for a TED Talk that nobody asked for.

Don't be that person. Nobody remembers the epic 12-minute monologue about your cat's digestive issues. What they remember is the *punchy, clear, on-point* contribution that cut through the noise.

So yes — earn your airtime. But don't confuse airtime with airspace. Speak with gravity, not volume.

***

Being heard isn't about begging for attention or bulldozing your way in. It's about showing up with credibility, presence, and clarity. Listening gets you invited to the table. How you deliver once you're there decides whether anyone leans in — or checks their phone.

Reflection Prompt:
Quick jot → What's one phrase or gesture you use that might undercut your presence?

Medium reflection → Write about a time someone tuned you out. Was it credibility, presence, or noise competition?

Deep journaling → Journal a "Hook, Bridge, Land" you could use in a high-stakes moment.

Next up: let's talk about listening in one-on-one conversations, where the stakes are often highest and the micro-signals matter most..

Part IV

Context & Dynamics

Here's where things get real. Conflict. Crisis. High-stakes conversations where a single misstep can escalate things. And also — the conversations we have with ourselves, which can be just as messy. This part is about listening when it matters most: when emotions are hot, stakes are high, or the voice in your own head won't shut up. You'll learn tools like the three-second pause, "name it to tame it," and journaling prompts to turn even the hardest listening moments into turning points.

Chapter 7

Listening In-Person (One-on-One)

The: I'm Fine Lie

We've all been there: you ask your friend, partner, or coworker how they're doing, and they answer with the most suspicious two words in the English language: *"I'm fine."*

Their mouths say "fine," but their bodies say: clenched jaw, arms folded like Fort Knox, eyes darting anywhere but yours. Translation? They are not fine. They are probably a Category 5 emotional hurricane dressed in business casual.

And yet, most of us nod, say, "Cool, glad to hear it," and move on — because we were listening with our ears, not our whole bodies.

In big groups, you can hide behind noise. But in one-on-one conversations, every flicker of your expression, every subtle shift in posture, every second of silence *matters*. This is where "whole-body listening" comes in: you don't just hear the words, you *read* the speaker.

The goal isn't to play FBI interrogator — it's to actually pay attention in a way that makes the other person feel seen. Which, by the way, is the fastest shortcut to a genuine connection.

The Research: The Power (and Pitfalls) of Micro-Expressions

Psychologist Paul Ekman, who essentially pioneered the study of micro-expressions (those lightning-fast flashes of emotion that reveal what we're really feeling), found that people unconsciously reveal the truth in their faces for just a fraction of a second. Fear, anger, sadness — it flickers, then it's gone.

Trained observers can spot these like neon signs, and even if you're not Ekman-level, you *can* get better at noticing. Why? Because communication is overwhelmingly non-verbal. Studies suggest that words make up less than 10% of what we interpret in a conversation; the rest comprises tone, posture, and expression.

But here's the catch: nonverbal "truth" is not a universal truth.

- People smile when they're nervous.

- Some cultures consider direct eye contact rude; others see it as respect.

- Even the FBI and TSA have been called out for overconfidence in "reading" micro-expressions — sometimes getting it flat-out wrong.

The actual skill isn't playing human lie detector. It's combining what you see with what you *know* about the person. Familiarity matters: if you already know your best friend smiles when they're hurting, you're more likely to interpret it correctly. In a new relationship? Sometimes the smarter move is to take people at their word until you've earned enough history to read between the lines.

And even when you *do* know someone well, tread lightly. Calling out, "I can tell you're lying" or "You're obviously upset," can feel invasive and backfire. Sometimes people need space before they're ready to admit what their face gave away.

Bottom line: Micro-expressions are powerful clues, not courtroom evidence. Use them as a prompt to stay curious, not a weapon to press harder.

So yes, your ears are important — but your eyes, your gut, and your willingness to pay attention matter just as much.

Sidebar: When the Rules Don't Apply

Everything we've covered about leaning in, nodding, decoding expressions — it's useful. But here's the catch: not everyone's brain or body plays by the same rules.

ADHD (Attention Deficit Hyperactivity Disorder): Someone with ADHD might interrupt you mid-sentence. Not because they don't care, but because their brain is juggling five thoughts at once and they know one will slip away if they don't blurt it out. On the flip side, they might hyper-focus — giving you laser-like attention that puts "good listeners" to shame.[10]

ASD (Autism Spectrum Disorder): A person on the spectrum may not show the facial cues or body language you expect. They may avoid eye contact or keep a flat expression even when deeply

---

[10] Brown, T. E. (2013). *A New Understanding of ADHD in Children and Adults: Executive Function Impairments.* Routledge.

engaged. Interpreting them through a "typical" lens can make you miss what they're really saying. Words matter more than eyebrow raises.[11]

Masking: Many neurodivergent people get so good at "masking" — forcing themselves to mirror typical cues — that they leave conversations exhausted. Respecting their listening style means taking what they say at face value rather than over-analyzing whether they smiled in the right place.[12]

The takeaway? Don't be a body-language detective with everyone. For some people, especially those who process differently, the safest way to listen is the simplest: hear their words, validate them, and resist the urge to decode like Sherlock Holmes on a sugar high.

Practical Tools: Noticing, Not Diagnosing

Want to elevate your one-on-one listening skills? Don't think of yourself as a lie detector. Think of yourself as a *pattern spotter*. Your goal isn't to call people out — it's to notice when something feels off and get curious (gently).

Here are five "possible mismatch" cues to practice noticing. Use them as yellow flags, not verdicts.

1.   **The Smile-Frown Combo.** Mouth says happy, eyes say nope. It could be discomfort or a habit. File it under: "Something more might be going on."

------

[11] American Psychiatric Association. (2013). *Diagnostic and Statistical Manual of Mental Disorders* (5th ed.).

[12] Kapp, S. K., et al. (2019). "Deficit, difference, or both? Autism and neurodiversity." *Developmental Psychology, 55*(1), 53–70

2. **The Shrink-Back.** They say, "I'm eager!" but their body leans away. Maybe it's nerves. Maybe it's sarcasm. Either way, the body language is worth a second thought. You could try, "Are you sure you are okay with this?"

3. **The Armoured Chest.** Crossed arms + stiff shoulders while claiming, "I'm open to feedback." Sometimes it's defensiveness; sometimes it's just cold in the room. You could try, "Would it help if I gave a specific example?"

4. **The Speedy Blink.** Rapid blinking paired with "I'm totally calm." Maybe stress, maybe dry contacts. Notice it; don't over-read it. You could slow the pace, lower your tone, and allow them to mirror you.

5. **The Fake Chill Voice.** The words are relaxed, but the tone is clipped or higher-pitched than usual. Could signal tension — or just too much coffee.

How to use this:

- **Notice:** See/hear the mismatch.

- **Pause:** Don't rush to judge.

- **Reflect:** Does this line up with what you know about this person?

- **Explore (gently):** If the relationship is close enough, try something like, *"I hear you saying X, but I'm picking up a different vibe. Want to talk about it?"*

The Golden Rule: Contradictions are invitations, not verdicts. You're not proving someone wrong; you're noticing clues that might deserve curiosity later.

Listening with Your Whole Body

Most people think "reading body language" is about scanning the other person like a human MRI machine. However, your body language is also speaking volumes. A lot. If you're slouched, arms crossed, scrolling through Instagram while someone's pouring their heart out, guess what? You just told them everything they need to know about how much you care: not much.

Whole-body listening isn't just about catching their signals — it's about managing your own so you're encouraging, not shutting down. You're not just a pair of ears. You're a full-body antenna broadcasting presence, empathy, and attention.

Here's how to practice whole-body listening:

- **Eyes:** Keep them on the speaker (without creepy staring). Notice shifts in expression.

- **Ears:** Track tone and pace. People speed up when anxious, slow down when thoughtful.

- **Body:** Angle toward them. Mirror, gently. Nod, but don't bobblehead.

- **Mind:** Stay present. Don't plan your next line — just *be there*.

- **Gut:** Trust it. If something feels "off," it probably is. Follow up with curiosity: "You said you're fine, but you seem a little tense — want to talk about it?"

Zip Zone: The Human Lie Detector Myth

Let's be clear — you don't need to morph into a lie detector robot. You'll drive yourself (and everyone else) insane if you treat every twitch as a secret confession. Sometimes an eye roll is just an eye roll. Sometimes "I'm fine" means, miraculously, they're actually fine.

The point isn't to bust people like you're auditioning for *Lie to Me*. The point is to listen with enough attention that when someone needs you to catch what they *can't say out loud,* you do.

***

Whole-body listening is about catching the moments in between the words. It's about slowing down long enough to see the real story hiding under "I'm fine." If you can tune into those signals without turning into a human polygraph, you'll deepen every one-on-one conversation you have.

And here's the kicker: once you master it in one-on-one settings, you'll be ready to apply the same principles in groups — where listening gets harder, louder, and more competitive.

Reflection Prompt:
Quick jot → Think of the last time someone said "I'm fine" when they weren't. What tipped you off?

Medium reflection → Which non-verbal cues do you notice most easily – facial expressions, body language, or tone shifts?

Deep journaling → Journal about a time when you misread someone's signals. How could you have slowed down or asked better questions?

Chapter 8

Listening in Groups & Teams

Brainstorming Chaos

Picture this: you're in a team brainstorming session. Whiteboard markers squeak, Post-its fly, everyone's talking over each other about "synergy," and somehow Bob is pitching an idea about drones even though you're trying to solve a supply-chain problem.

Welcome to group dynamics — where listening doesn't just get harder, it gets competitive. And if one-on-one listening is like learning to swim, group listening is like trying to stay afloat in a wave pool at peak summer hours.

Why Group Listening is Its Own Beast

Here's the problem: in groups, people don't just aspire to be heard — they want to stand out. And when everyone's jockeying for airtime, actual listening plummets.

The irony? Teams often mistake noise for productivity. Just because 20 ideas hit the table in two minutes doesn't mean anyone's absorbing them. Real collaboration only happens when people feel both heard *and* understood.

The One-Upper: The Café Saboteur

Now let's talk about the *one-upper*. You know the type. You're out at a café with four friends, telling a story about how you sprained your ankle on a hike. Before you can finish, here comes One-Upper: *"That's nothing — I once broke my leg in three places while BASE jumping in Switzerland."*

These people don't mean to be villains, but their conversational style has a way of sucking the air out of the room. They shift the spotlight rather than sharing it, which erodes group trust. In teams, the one-upper can derail conversations, making others feel invisible and overlooked.

Tip: Instead of fighting them, acknowledge their story ("Wow, that sounds intense") and gently bring the spotlight back ("Okay, but let's circle back to Jordan's point about...") — a move that re-centres the group.

Practical Tools for Group Listening

1. **Group Radar Technique**

   Imagine a radar screen with blips representing each person's input. In groups, your job isn't just to track your own "signal" but to scan the radar for quieter voices. Ask: *Who hasn't spoken yet? Whose ideas keep getting cut off?* Bringing those voices in makes you a group-listening MVP.

2. **Meeting Listening Map**

   Try sketching a quick "listening map" during discussions. Write each speaker's name and their core point. This prevents idea amnesia (when three people say the same thing and nobody notices) and helps ensure you're absorbing, not just waiting to talk.

3. **The Pause Button**

In group chaos, silence is your secret weapon. Don't pile on the noise — pause, then paraphrase what you just heard: *"Okay, I'm hearing two themes: A and B. Did I get that right?"* Boom. Instant clarity.

Zip Zone: Zoom Call Madness

And of course, no chapter on group listening would be complete without addressing Zoom calls. We've all lived this nightmare:

- Six people talking at once.

- One person frozen mid-word.

- Someone muted, miming frantically.

- The inevitable "No, you go ahead—no, you go—no, you."

If Dante were alive today, he'd add "Endless Zoom Brainstorm" as the tenth circle of hell.

Quick Quiz: Are You the One-Upper?

Answer yes/no to these questions:

1. When someone shares a story, do you immediately think of how your experience compares?

2. Do you often start responses with "That reminds me of when I..."?

3. Do people sometimes sigh or glaze over when you jump in?

4. Have you ever accidentally hijacked a meeting to talk about yourself?

5. Do you feel a powerful urge to "top" whatever's being said?

Scoring:

- 0–1 Yes: You're safe. You know how to share airtime.

- 2–3 Yes: You're in danger of one-upping. Awareness is half the battle.

- 4–5 Yes: Congratulations, you're the café saboteur. The good news? You can reform. Start practicing the phrase, *"Tell me more about that."*

***

Listening in groups isn't about being the loudest voice; it's about creating space so that ideas can actually take hold. Whether it's taming the chaos of a brainstorm, gently redirecting a one-upper, or mapping conversations so they don't get lost in the noise, successful group listeners are the unsung heroes of collaboration.

Because in the end, nobody remembers the person who shouted the most. They remember the person who made everyone else feel heard.

Reflection Prompt:

Quick jot → Who dominates in your group settings? Who gets ignored?

Medium reflection → Which role do you play more often: the one-upper, the talker, or the quiet observer?

Deep journaling → Write about a time you redirected attention to someone quieter. How did the group dynamic shift

Chapter 9

Listening Without Visuals (Social Media, Text, Email)

The Multitask Disaster

Picture this: you're on a tense client call, trying to sound engaged while secretly firing off a "quick" email. You think you're pulling it off — but then the client stops mid-sentence and asks, *"Are you... still there?"* Busted.

Here's the reality: without visuals, your listening has to work harder. You don't get the crutch of nods, smiles, or sympathetic eyebrow raises. All you've got is tone, timing, and text — and those can betray you just as easily as they can save you.

Practical Fixes:

- **Remove temptation.** If you tend to get distracted easily, consider shutting down your email, putting your phone in another room, or closing Slack. Don't set yourself up for failure.

- **Record when possible.** If you're worried about missing details, ask: *"Mind if I record this so I can give you my full attention?"* Recording frees your mind from the stress of frantic note-taking.

- **Signal engagement verbally.** Since you can't nod, drop brief acknowledgments ("Got it," "That makes sense," "I see what you're saying") — but sparingly, or you'll sound like a bad chatbot.

Notification Hell: The Death of Deep Listening

Here's the thing about modern life: it's not that we don't want to listen — it's that our phones, laptops, and watches have basically conspired to make it impossible. You can have the best of intentions on a client call, a heart-to-heart with your partner, or a casual "how was your day?" — and still, ding, buzz, ping, swoosh — your attention is gone.

You don't even need to check the notifications. Your brain already left the conversation and sprinted over to the imaginary messaging tool. Neuroscientists have demonstrated that even the presence of a silent phone on the table can reduce attention and empathy levels during conversations.[13] Why? Because part of your brain is constantly whispering, What if it's important? Spoiler: it's probably a DoorDash coupon.

This is what I call Notification Hell—the constant background noise of digital life that keeps us from going deep. And the cruel irony? We think we're "multitasking" like productivity ninjas, but every ping slices our focus into smaller and smaller chunks. Research from the University of California, Irvine, found that it can take over 23 minutes to fully refocus after a digital interruption.[14] Twenty-three

[13] Thornton, B., Faires, A., Robbins, M., & Rollins, E. (2014). *The mere presence of a cell phone may be distracting.* Social Psychology, 45(6), 479–488.

[14] Mark, G., Gudith, D., & Klocke, U. (2008). The cost of interrupted work: More speed and stress. Proceedings of the SIGCHI Conference on Human Factors in Computing Systems, 107–110.

minutes! That means every Slack ping is essentially setting your brain on fire and then leaving you to extinguish the flames.

So if you've ever wondered why your conversations feel shallow, why your kid says, "Never mind, you're not listening," or why your client thinks you're checked out — it's not always you. Sometimes it's your damn notifications.

The Notification Hygiene Checklist

Here's how to climb out of Notification Hell and give people (and yourself) the gift of full presence:

1. **Batch Notifications**
   Turn off push alerts for everything except emergencies. Email? You don't need to know the second Aunt Karen replies "LOL" to the family chain. Check it in blocks.
2. **Slack (or Teams) Boundaries**
   Set "Do Not Disturb" windows during deep work or important calls. Most platforms even let you announce: *"Back at 3:00."* Use it. Otherwise, you're just inviting the chaos gremlins in.
3. **Phone Out of Arm's Reach**
   Don't just silence your phone — exile it. If possible, put it in another room. If that's not possible, flip the screen down and out of sight. Out of sight really does mean out of mind.
4. **Focus Modes Are Your Friend**
   Both iOS and Android offer customizable Focus or Do Not Disturb settings. Create one for "Conversations" that only lets through actual humans who can set your house on fire — everyone else can wait.

5. **Stop Worshipping the Smartwatch**

   Look, I love my watch too. But if it buzzes every three seconds, you're basically strapping anxiety to your wrist. Either turn off non-essential notifications or accept that your wrist is now the most distracting object in the room.

The Tone Problem

Can you "read with tone"? Absolutely — but it's a dangerous game. Take this line: *Mary had a little lamb.*

- *Mary* had a little lamb (Not Susan, don't get it twisted).

- Mary *had* a little lamb (Ownership? Or a tragic *had*?).

- Mary had a *little* lamb (Not big, not medium, just fun-sized).

- Mary had a little *lamb* (As opposed to, say, a goat).

Same words, wildly different meanings. This is the problem with text-based communication: readers inject their own tone, their own baggage, their own "Mary." No wonder so many texts and emails blow up into arguments.

Practical Fixes:

- **When in doubt, add context.** Emojis, brackets, or a clarifying sentence can prevent hours of misinterpretation. (*"That's fine 😊"* vs. *"That's fine."* = *two different universes.*)

- **Don't litigate tone over text.** If something feels loaded, hop on the phone. Ask: *"Hey, just to make sure I understood that right — can we talk this through quickly?"*

- **Check your own sends.** Reread your email/text, imagining you're in a bad mood. If it sounds harsher than you intended, soften it before hitting send.

Memes: Modern Listening or Just Noise?

Here's a thought: memes might be the modern world's desperate attempt to be heard in a culture drowning in words. They distil meaning, emotion, and humour into a single image + line combo.

- You send the crying Michael Jordan face; your friend gets you instantly.

- You drop the distracted boyfriend meme; suddenly, you're having a full commentary on priorities.

Are memes a "real" form of listening? Maybe. At a minimum, they're shorthand signals that say: *I saw you. I feel this too. Here's our shared language.* In a way, it's empathy with a punchline.

Practical Fixes:

- **Know your audience.** Memes land when you share a cultural context. Send the wrong one, and you risk looking flippant.

- **Don't replace words entirely.** Memes work best as seasoning, not the entire meal. Pair them with at least a sentence of genuine acknowledgment.

- **Use them as bridges.** A meme can lighten tension and open the door to a deeper talk ("Okay, but seriously, how are you holding up?").

Practical Tool: The "Echo, Clarify, and Reset" Method

When you don't have visuals, you need to triple down on presence. Try this three-part sequence:

1. Echo → Paraphrase what you heard.

   - Example: *"So you're saying the deadline feels unrealistic?"* This reassures the other person that they weren't lost in the digital void.

2. Clarify → Ask for specifics before assuming.

   - Example: *"When you say urgent, do you mean by the end of today or the end of the week?"*

3. Reset → If you missed something (hello, multitasking guilt), own it and re-engage.

   - Example: *"Sorry, I lost track there for a second — can you repeat the part about the client's timeline?"* (Obviously, don't pull this for the easy stuff like, *"What are you doing this weekend?"* That just makes you look checked out.)

Lesson: The best "reset" is prevention. If you're listening halfway, you're not really listening.

Zip Zone: Bad Listening in Text Form

If you've ever tried to pour your heart out while someone nods along *to their phone,* you know how soul-crushing this is. Don't be that person. Nobody ever looked back and said, *"Wow, I'm so glad I split my attention between my kid's first heartbreak and a fantasy football update."*

Quick Exercise: Tone Check

Choose a recent text or email where the tone felt off. Now do this:

1. Rewrite it three different ways, emphasizing different words or inserting different punctuation.

2. Notice how the meaning shifts.

3. Before sending your next message, ask: *How could this be read wrong?* and tweak it to reduce the risk.

Bonus: Try replying to one message today using the "Echo and Clarify" method. See if the other person's response gets warmer or clearer.

Case Study: Giving Space vs. Pushing Too Hard

My son has ASD Type 1 (Autism Spectrum Disorder), formerly referred to as Asperger's. Emotional regulation has always been a challenge for him, and articulating feelings at the moment is even harder. My mother, bless her, isn't wired for patience when she senses something's wrong. She presses: *"Come on, I can tell something's wrong."*

The result? He doesn't shout it out; he gets physically abusive to himself. He'll hit his head, pull at his hair, and his face turns red. It's heartbreaking, but it's not because he doesn't want to talk. It's because he literally *can't* in that moment. The pressure to perform emotionally just short-circuits him.

Through trial (and lots of error), I've learned something else works: giving him space. When I sense something's off, I say: *"Hey, bud, I feel like something might be bothering you. We can talk about it later if you like, maybe after dinner."*

Different result, every time. No meltdown. Just a little processing time. Later, he'll circle back — calmer, clearer, and ready to share.

The Lesson: Not everyone can "talk it out" on your timeline. Respecting the "Not now" creates the safety someone needs to say eventually, "Okay, here's what's wrong."

Why My Trial and Error Method Works—Apparently Science

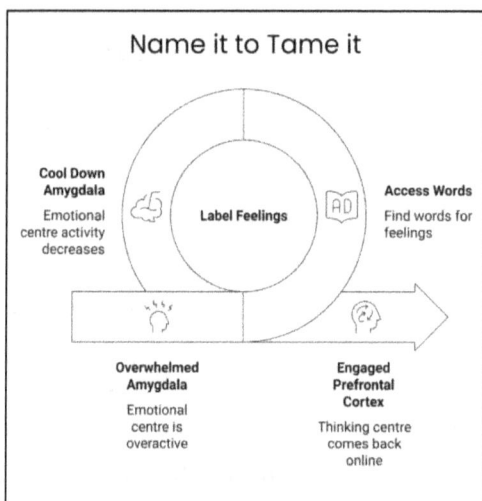

Name it to Tame it

Cool Down
Amygdala
Emotional centre activity decreases

Access Words
Find words for feelings

Label Feelings

Overwhelmed Amygdala
Emotional centre is overactive

Engaged Prefrontal Cortex
Thinking centre comes back online

Neuroscience backs this up. Dr. Dan Siegel calls it the *"name it to tame it"* principle: when people can label their feelings, the brain's emotional centre (the amygdala) cools down, and the thinking centre (the prefrontal cortex) comes back online. But people with ASD and other regulation challenges often need more time to access the words that fit their feelings.

Research on ASD and processing delays (e.g., Mazefsky et al., 2013, *Emotion Regulation in Autism Spectrum Disorder*) shows that forcing immediate responses can overwhelm the system, leading to meltdowns instead of clarity.

One method with children is to ask questions like, 'What colour(s) are you feeling?' Where in your body do you feel your emotions? If your emotions could make a noise, what noise would it be? Let the senses explain the emotions instead of labels.

Even outside of ASD, psychologist Paul Ekman's research on emotional leakage demonstrates that when emotions can't be expressed verbally, they'll often come out in the body — gestures, tension, or physical outbursts.

So whether you're parenting, partnering, or managing a team, the science is clear: listening to what's *not said yet* can be more powerful than bulldozing for an answer now.

***

Listening without visuals means you don't have the safety net of body language to rely on. Instead, you must be intentional with your words, timing, and empathy. Whether it's echoing back in a phone call, clarifying over email, or — yes — using the perfect meme to say *I hear you,* the goal is the same: make people feel understood even when they can't see your face.

Reflection Prompt:
Quick jot → How many times did you check notifications in your last meeting?

Medium reflection → Write one digital "echo and clarify" line you could use ("Just to make sure I understood···").

Deep journaling → Reflect on a text/email you misinterpreted. How did tone distort meaning, and how could you prevent that next time?

Part V

Pressure Tested & Practiced

Enough theory. This is the lab portion of the book — where you get to practice, experiment, and mess up in safe ways. You'll find role-plays, challenges, scripts, and even some celebrity case studies (Oprah: gold star. Certain late-night disasters: cautionary tale). This part is about testing yourself, stretching your listening muscles, and seeing how much changes when you really put it all into play. By the end, you won't just know how to listen — you'll be living it.

Chapter 10

High-Stakes Listening

When Silence Feels Safer

There's a reason some people shut down in heated conversations: talking feels like tossing a match into a fireworks factory. You say one wrong thing, and *boom*—everything explodes.

Picture this: you're in a relationship fight where every sentence is a booby trap. You start with, *"I feel like you don't..."* and before you can finish, the other person cuts you off with, *"Oh, here we go again."* Your brain slams on the brakes. Why risk setting off another round of fireworks? Silence feels safer.

But sometimes silence doesn't come from fear of explosion. It comes from futility. You speak up, but your words vanish into the ether while the person across from you hijacks the moment. Think: a team meeting where you finally weigh in, only to be immediately steamrolled by the loudest voice in the room. That silence you fall into? That's not peace. That's surrender.

Welcome to high-stakes listening: when emotions are running hot, words carry weight, and one bad response can wreck trust for years.

The Stakes Are Higher Than You Think

We tend to think "high-stakes" means hostage negotiations, political summits, or a viral celebrity interview meltdown. And yeah, those matter. Fun fact: FBI hostage negotiators are trained to spend 80% of their time listening, not talking. Imagine if your boss tried that in a staff meeting. Revolutionary.

But here's the secret: *your* high-stakes moments happen every damn day.

- When your partner finally admits something's wrong.

- When your teenager mutters, "I don't want to talk about it."

- When a colleague blurts out, "I can't do this anymore."

- When you open up about something personal and the other person… doesn't hear you.

The stakes aren't measured by body counts. They're measured by trust, dignity, and whether someone feels seen in their most vulnerable moment.

When Power Dynamics Explode in High-Stakes Conversations

Here's the thing about high-stakes listening: it doesn't just crank up emotions — it cranks up hierarchies. When the pressure is on, the loudest voice often hijacks the room, and the quieter but crucial perspectives get drowned out.

Think about a heated team crisis call: deadlines slipping, clients panicking. The manager with the most authority storms in, starts directing traffic, and everyone else shuts down. Who actually knows the root cause? They stay silent. Why? Because high stakes and power imbalances lead to silence feeling safer than speaking up.

Psychological safety [15] , a concept Amy Edmondson hammered into leadership culture, is never more fragile than during a crisis. When people fear their input will be punished, dismissed, or bulldozed, they withhold. And here's the kicker: the information you most need in a crisis is often the thing only the quietest person in the room can tell you.

The Redirect Move

So how do you break the "loudest wins" trap? Try the redirect move.

It's the crisis cousin to the "Power Flip" from Chapter 6.

1. **Acknowledge the Noise**
   - "I hear a lot of energy right now. Let's pause before we bulldoze over each other."
2. **Call on the Quiet Voice**
   - "I want to hear from Sam — you've been closest to the data. What's your take?"
   - "Maria, you've been quiet, but I know you've been tracking this. What are you seeing?"
3. **Protect the Space**

---

[15] Edmondson, A. (1999). *Psychological safety and learning behavior in work teams.* Administrative Science Quarterly, 44(2), 350–383.

Don't just invite the voice — shield it. Stop interruptions until they're finished. If you have to, use your authority to hold the floor:

- "Let's let Sam finish before we react."

Case Study: NASA's Challenger Disaster

Before the Challenger launch in 1986, engineers at Morton Thiokol had serious concerns about O-ring failure in cold weather. But in the high-stakes meeting the night before the launch, NASA leadership pushed hard for a "go" decision. The quieter engineering voices were drowned out by the urgency to proceed. The result was catastrophic.[16]

This is the cost of ignoring power dynamics in crisis: the people with the knowledge may not have the authority — and without deliberate listening, their voices vanish.

Why We Blow It

So why do we screw up the listening game when it matters most?

1. We're addicted to fixing. Silence feels awkward, so we rush to fill it with solutions.

2. We centre ourselves. Your brain whispers, "How does this connect to *me*?" and suddenly you're telling your own story instead of holding space.

3. We panic. Emotions spike, and you grab control of the conversation like it's a runaway shopping cart.

---

[16] Vaughan, D. (1996). *The Challenger Launch Decision: Risky Technology, Culture, and Deviance at NASA*. University of Chicago Press.

4. We don't respect silence. We treat pauses as problems instead of power.

As we reviewed previously, we cannot have our listening superpower on all the time. We have to turn it off to recharge it. Contextual listening is the key. Activate your active listening skills and assess the situation. Do you need to move into empathetic, or can you dip back down into passive listening for a bit?

Borrowing from Hostage Negotiators

Here's where the FBI comes in. Hostage negotiators are trained for situations where one wrong word could get someone killed. Their golden rules?

- **Active Listening** → Repeat key phrases back. ("It sounds like you're feeling trapped.")

- **Emotional Labelling** → Name the emotion they're showing. ("You're angry. You feel cornered.")

- **Silence as a Tool** → Don't rush. Let the person fill the space when they're ready.

- **The 3-Second Pause** → Before responding, breathe, count to three, *then* speak.

If these techniques can prevent someone from pulling the trigger, they can also prevent your marriage, workplace, or Thanksgiving dinner from going nuclear.

Practical Tools

1. The 3-Second Pause

- Hear something intense? Stop.

- Inhale. Count one... two... three.

- Only then do you respond.

This does two things: lowers your own emotional reactivity and signals respect. You're not rushing to dismiss, fix, or hijack. You're holding space.

2. Script: Acknowledgment Without Hijacking

Instead of:

- "Oh, the same thing happened to me—" (Nope, shut it.)

- "Don't worry, it'll be fine." (Translation: stop feeling that.)

  Try:

- "That sounds heavy."

- "I want to understand more. Tell me what that's like."

- "I hear you. Do you want me to listen, or help problem-solve?"

3. Survival Plan for Not Being Heard

What if *you're* the one ignored, like my neck-breaking story? Here's how to reclaim your voice without burning bridges:

- **Call It Out Calmly**: "I just shared something important, and it feels like it got missed."

- **Re-centre the Conversation**: "Before we move on, I'd like to finish my thought."

- **Follow up Later** (if the moment is lost): "When I mentioned my injury earlier, it felt overlooked. It's important to me that you know what happened."

4. When to Shut Up

Sometimes the bravest move is silence. Not sulking silence —
the intentional kind.

- When someone's spiralling, hold back and let them breathe.

- When emotions are raw, offer, "We can talk later if you
  want."

- When you're triggered, admit it: "I need a second to regroup
  before I respond."

***

High-stakes listening isn't about being the hero with the
perfect comeback. It's about resisting the urge to fix, hijack, or panic,
and instead creating a pause where trust can breathe.

If FBI negotiators can use silence to save hostages, you can use
it to save your marriage, your friendship, or your sanity.

Remember this: the next time someone hands you their heart,
don't drop it. Count to three.

Reflection Prompt:

Quick jot → Recall the last conflict you were in. Did you pause before responding?

Medium reflection → Which phrase escalates you most when someone else uses it (e.g., "Calm down")? How could you defuse instead of react?

Deep journaling → Write about a high-stakes moment you wish you could redo. What 3-second pause, question, or silence might have shifted it?

Chapter 11

Shut Up and Listen to Yourself

This isn't just about self-care. Listening to yourself is the secret ingredient that makes every other chapter work. You can't mirror someone else's emotions if you're blind to your own. You can't stay present in a heated argument if your inner monologue is screaming louder than the other person. And you can't keep showing up for others without burning out unless you first show up for yourself.

You've probably heard this advice before: "Trust your gut." Or, "Listen to your inner voice." Easy to say. But what if your inner voice doesn't sound like Morgan Freeman narrating your wisdom? What if it's more like a caffeinated auctioneer, firing thoughts at lightning speed, or worse — a toddler on a sugar high who won't stop yelling, "Listen to me! LISTEN TO ME!"

Most of us have an internal monologue. For some, it's background commentary, like elevator music you hardly notice. For others — especially if you are neurodivergent — it's a full surround-sound system. Psychologists call this inner speech[17]. It helps us plan,

---

[17] Morin, A. (2009). *Inner speech and consciousness.* In P. Wilken, A. Cleeremans, & Y. Rossetti (Eds.), *Neuropsychology of Consciousness* (pp. 203–233). Psychology Press.

solve problems, and process emotions. But when we ignore it, that monologue doesn't just fade away. It gets louder and more chaotic until it throws a temper tantrum that hijacks your attention.

That's why "listening to yourself" isn't some fluffy self-care poster. It's survival. If you don't give your thoughts airtime on your terms, they'll take the mic on theirs.

The Inner Monologue: Your Brain's Unpaid Podcaster

My inner monologue has ever-changing accents. Depending on my latest Audible binge, I'll catch myself thinking in a heavy Scottish accent or narrating life like a noir detective. It's quirky, sure, but it's also proof that my brain never shuts up. Yours probably doesn't either.

Researchers Alderson-Day & Fernyhough found that inner speech shows up in nearly everyone, but the way we experience it varies[18]. Some people receive motivational pep talks, others receive harsh criticism, and some are given endless to-do lists that scroll like a teleprompter. For folks with ADHD, that voice tends to hyper-fixate — replaying one worry on loop. For autistic thinkers, it can be a way to process social confusion or rehearse interactions.

Bottom line: everyone's got a version of this, and ignoring it is like letting your inbox pile up until it bursts.

---

[18] Alderson-Day, B., & Fernyhough, C. (2015). *Inner speech: Development, cognitive functions, phenomenology, and neurobiology. Psychological Bulletin, 141*(5), 931–965.

The Inner Listening Spectrum

Remember the listening spectrum from earlier? Passive →
Active → Empathic → Strategic. The same framework works inward,
too. Your brain throws out dozens of thoughts an hour. Not all of
them deserve a full therapy session.

- Passive Inner Listening—Most thoughts live here. Acknowledge
  them, then move on.

  Example: "Did I turn off the stove?" Passive listening = quick
  scan, then let it go.

- Active Inner Listening—When a thought keeps circling, engage
  it. Ask why.

  Example: "I keep replaying that awkward thing I said." Active
  listening = "Am I embarrassed about the moment, or is this
  about feeling undervalued overall?"

- Empathic Inner Listening—For the heavy emotions. Sit with
  them; don't brush them off.

  Example: "I feel like a crappy parent." Empathic listening =
  "That hurts. I hear you. Let's sit here for a bit."

- Strategic Inner Listening—For signals that require action.

  Example: "I get anxious every Sunday night." Strategic listening
  = "That's not random. That's pointing to a bigger issue with
  work. Time to address it."

The trick is balance: don't passive-listen to everything, but
don't strategic-listen yourself into exhaustion either.

93

Audit Your Thoughts Like Conversations

Next time your brain spins up, try this: pretend you're listening to a friend. Place the thought on the spectrum. Is it a quick nod-and-release moment (passive)? A clarifying question (active)? A hug-and-sit-with-it moment (empathic)? Or a nudge toward action (strategic)?

Not every thought deserves full attention. Knowing which listening mode to use helps you avoid getting lost in your own thoughts.

Whole-Body Inner Listening with a Mirror

Listening isn't just about hearing; it's about being present. The same goes for listening to yourself. One of the best hacks? Try it in front of a mirror.

- Lean In: Literally lean toward yourself. Notice how it feels. Are you showing up with curiosity or critique?
- Make eye contact: Look yourself in the eyes. Do you flinch, avoid, or soften? That's data.
- Scan the tension: jaw clenched? Shoulders up? That's your body speaking louder than words.
- Notice the fidgets: the tapping, the shifting, the crossed arms — would you ignore those cues in a friend? Don't ignore them in yourself.

It feels weird at first (borderline cringe, honestly), but it's powerful. By treating yourself as both speaker and listener, you practice giving your inner voice the same respect you'd give anyone else.

How to Give Your Inner Voice the Floor (Without Letting It Take Over)

Pause Before the Tantrum

Think of your monologue like a toddler. If you don't look it in the eye and say, "Okay, what do you need?" it'll throw itself on the grocery store floor until you can't ignore it. Catch it early. Pause once or twice a day and ask: *What's the loudest voice in my head right now?*

Name the Theme

Don't get lost in word-for-word translation. Summarize.

- Monologue: "Why did I say that in the meeting? They must think I'm an idiot."

- Translation: *I feel insecure about how I came across.*

- Monologue: "Deadline. Deadline. Deadline. You're behind!"

- Translation: *I'm anxious about my workload.*

When you label the theme, you take the sting out. Neuroscience supports this finding: naming an emotion calms the amygdala, the part of the brain responsible for the fight-or-flight response (Lieberman et al., 2007).

Let It Talk — With Boundaries

You don't have to indulge a 20-minute TED Talk in your skull. Give your thoughts a stage, but keep the spotlight brief. Try journaling one paragraph that starts with, "What I really want to say is…" or voice-memo your brain dump while driving. Then stop.

Reply Like You Would to a Friend

Your monologue isn't just noise; it's communication. Treat it the way you'd treat someone ranting at coffee. Listen. Validate. Redirect.

- Thought: "I'll never get this done."

- Response: "You're overwhelmed. Okay. What's the *first* step?"

Document, Reflect, Repeat

Journaling isn't about writing poetry. It's about creating a feedback loop with yourself. Write what's circling in your head. Re-read later. See the patterns. This is how you turn listening inward into understanding yourself.

Beyond Journalling:

Voice Notes: Talk to yourself out loud for 60 seconds. Listening back can reveal patterns you missed (tone, repetition, hidden emotions).

Mirror Check: Stand in front of the mirror for 2 minutes after a hard conversation. Watch your body language: Are you tense, slouched, or avoiding eye contact? That's the feedback you need.

5-Minute Inner Debrief: After tough conversations, ask:

- What did I feel?
- What did I hear?

- What do I wish I'd said?

This rewires your brain to process, not suppress.

Neurodiverse Hacks: If you've got ADHD or ASD, externalizing thoughts (writing, recording, doodling) isn't optional – it's essential. Otherwise, your brain loops until it wins the volume war.

Zip Zone

If you never listen to yourself, your monologue will eventually stage a coup — hijacking your focus during meetings, conversations, or at 2 a.m. when you desperately want sleep. Better to give it the mic on your terms.

Reflection Prompt:
Quick jot → What's the loudest theme in your inner monologue this week?

Medium reflection → When do you ignore yourself most often — during work, family life, or downtime?

Deep journaling → Journal about a moment you finally listened to yourself (gut feeling, intuition). How did it change your decision?

Chapter 12

When Your Brain Won't Shut Up

Ever lie in bed, lights off, body ready to sleep... and your brain decides it's auditioning for a TED Talk? Cue nonstop loop: "Why did I say that joke in 2012?" or "What if they think I suck at presentations?" That endless chatter isn't just background noise—it hijacks your presence in every conversation that follows.

Welcome to your default broadcast: your own brain, live 24/7. And today, we reclaim the remote.

Why the Mental Static Feels Endless

- **The Default Mode Network (DMN):** This brain network powers mind wandering, self-reflection, and future planning. Great when you want creativity. Dangerous when it runs on autopilot.[19]

- **Negativity Bias:** Your brain evolved to flag threats—real or imagined. That means the one negative thought dings me louder than ten "you're okay" signals.

- **Modern Trigger Overload:** The phone never stops. The inbox never empties. If you never quiet your brain, it becomes the conductor of chaos.

---

[19] Menon, V. (2023). *20 years of the default mode network: A review and synthesis.* Neuron.

Mini-Story: Nightly Brain Interview

A friend told me about her nightly routine of self-sabotage. She'd crawl into bed, exhausted and ready to shut down, only to have her brain flip on like a stadium floodlight. Instead of rest, she got a 20-minute inquisition: *Why did you say that dumb thing in the meeting? Why haven't you called your sister back? How long before everyone realizes you're faking it at work?*

It was less "sweet dreams" and more "FBI interrogation."

Finally, she hacked it. She put a cheap notepad on her nightstand and made a deal with her brain: *Fine. You want to unload? Go ahead. But we're parking it here until morning.* Each spiralling thought got scribbled into the "Parking Lot" notebook. Her reassurance line? "We'll revisit this tomorrow."

Her brain actually bought it. Within a week, she was falling asleep instead of cross-examining herself nightly. Nothing mystical, just a simple system: capture it, contain it, and move on.

Not every trick works for everyone. For me? A "Parking Lot" would be a disaster. Give me a pad of paper by the bed, and suddenly I'm not offloading worries, I'm storyboarding. What was supposed to be five minutes of release turns into a midnight TED Talk written in bullet points until my fingers cramp.

So instead, I drew inspiration from yoga Nidra — the guided practice that's essentially a full-body meditation. I don't roll out a mat or light incense; I just shift my focus, piece by piece. Throat centre. Right shoulder. Right elbow. Right wrist. Thumb. Index finger. Back up to centre. Then down the left side. Chest, centre, chest. All without moving a muscle.

The magic is that the brain cannot simultaneously spiral and scan your body. The focus forces everything to relax. For me, that's how I shut the f*ck up at night: not by writing the noise down, but by giving my brain a different job.

Practical Tools to Mute the Noise

1. Tell Yourself to Shut the F*ck Up

- Function: acts like a mental circuit breaker.

- Why it works: It interrupts autopilot thinking with humour and force. Don't just think it—say it (even silently) and follow with a breath.

2. The Parking Lot

- Capture intrusive thoughts in a trusted container: a journal, notes app, or sticky notes. Once written, your brain relaxes—working memory is freed.

3. The Worry Appointment

- Set a daily 15-minute slot for worry fix. At the moment, tell your brain: *"Not now—see you at 7 p.m."* Research shows this builds trust in your brain to pause.[20]

4. Breath as Reset

- Technique: Inhale 4s—hold 4s—exhale 6–8s. Longer exhales trigger the parasympathetic system. Instantly hit the reset button.

5. Channel the Voice

---

[20] Verywell Mind. (2012). Journaling to cope with anxiety

- Don't fight it—mock it. Speak the intrusive thought in a silly accent or voice (think Kermit or Morgan Freeman). Humour strips it of power.

Case Study: From Overthinker to Confident Presenter

A client prepping for a big pitch couldn't stop ruminating: *"What if I freeze? What if I bomb?"* She used the Parking Lot + *shut the f*ck up mode* combo. She parked each worry, reigned in spirals with breath, then delivered the pitch—clear, calm, and confident. "Felt like I stopped overdosing on my own thoughts," she later said.

Reflection Prompts

- What's the loudest channel in your internal radio right now?

- If in 20 minutes you turned that volume down by just 30%, what would shift?

- Which one of these tools can you try *right now*—yes, even at this exact moment?

Why This Makes You a Better Listener?

When you quiet your internal noise:

- You're present—not reacting, but listening.

- You speak with clarity, not static.

- You empathize with space, not urgency.

Zip Zone

If you're auditioning your inner monologue for stand-up, fine—but don't serve it on someone else's plate expecting applause.

***

Your brain will chatter nonstop. That's its job. But you don't have to be a hostage to its noise. Whether with a sharp *"shut the f*ck up,"* a booked worry show, or a breath, you hold the mic. Calm brain = clear communication.

> **Reflection Prompt:**
> Quick jot → Write one recurring thought loop that drives you nuts.
>
> Medium reflection → Which tool helps you most to calm it (parking lot pad, yoga nidra focus, breathing, etc.)?
>
> Deep journaling → Journal about a night your brain hijacked your sleep. What was the thought's "temper tantrum," and how could you have given it audience earlier?

Chapter 13

Listening Labs — Exercises & Challenges

If listening were a sport, this is where you'd lace up your sneakers. You've read about listening styles, body language, silence, and even how to tell your brain to shut up—but none of it sticks unless you practice. This chapter serves as your personal gym for developing listening skills, offering safe spaces, role-plays, and challenges that push you to flex new muscles until they become second nature.

Think about the first time you tried yoga, or salsa dancing, or even playing an instrument. You didn't "get it" by reading the book—you had to stumble, wobble, and maybe step on someone's toes before you improved. Listening is no different. The point of a "lab" isn't perfection; it's experimenting in real life.

Role-Plays: Test Driving Conversations

Grab a partner (or two) and try these mini-scenes. The goal isn't to perform—it's noticing where you trip up and what it feels like to adjust.

1. **The Couples Script:**

    *   Partner A shares something annoying that happened at work.

    *   Partner B practices mirroring ("What I hear you saying is...") and resists the urge to fix.

    *   Switch roles.

    *   Debrief: Was it harder to resist advice than you thought?

2. **The Coworker Feedback Loop:**

    *   Partner A plays the "boss" giving vague feedback: "You need to be more proactive."

    *   Partner B listens, echoes back, and asks clarifying questions.

    *   Switch roles.

    *   Debrief: How did clarifying reshape the conversation?

3. **The Friend in Crisis:**

    *   Partner A pretends to dump bad news.

    *   Partner B listens without interrupting, then offers support using one sentence only.

    *   Debrief: Did silence feel uncomfortable? Did it change the energy?

Challenges: Listening Workouts You Can Do Solo

1. **24-Hour No-Interrupting Challenge**
    For one day, make it your mission not to cut anyone off. Notice how long people actually talk when you don't jump in. Spoiler: it's usually less than you think.

2. **Mirroring Marathon**
   In every conversation for one day, mirror back at least one phrase or feeling. Example: "Sounds like that was really frustrating." This isn't about parroting—it's about showing you *heard*.

3. **The Pause Button**
   In your next heated conversation, force yourself to wait three seconds before responding. This tiny pause can completely change the outcome. (Also a good hack if your mouth tends to outrun your brain.)

Conversation Templates

Sometimes we need a script to get unstuck. Here are a few "listening-first" conversation templates you can borrow:

- **Apologies**
  "I want to make sure I understand how I hurt you before I explain myself. Can you tell me what that felt like for you?"

- **Feedback**
  "Here's what I noticed. How did that land for you?"

- **Support**
  "It sounds like you're carrying a lot. Do you want me to just listen, or help you think through solutions?"

- **Boundaries**
  "I value our relationship, but I need to pause this conversation right now. Let's circle back when I can give it my full attention."

Zip Zone

Try the "silent Zoom box" game. In your next online meeting, mute yourself, turn your camera on, and practice *responding only with your* body language. See if your nods, smiles, and eyebrows can carry the conversation as much as your words.

Quiz: What's Your Listening Fitness Level?

- How often did you interrupt someone yesterday?
    - A) 0–1 times → Listener Olympian
    - B) 2–4 times → Weekend Warrior
    - C) Lost count → Needs training wheels
- In your last tough conversation, did you:
    - A) Mirror feelings at least once
    - B) Nod a lot but say nothing
    - C) Talk more than they did
- Do people thank you for listening?
    - A) Often
    - B) Sometimes
    - C) Never (ouch)

Scoring:
Mostly A's → Keep coaching others.
Mostly B's → Good instincts, but time to sharpen.
Mostly C's → Don't panic. Listening is a skill, not a personality trait. Start with one challenge above.

Role-Plays Revisited: Test Driving with Real Words

Earlier, you saw the setup. Now let's run through each scene in full, so you can "hear" how it might sound. These aren't perfect dialogues—they're deliberately ordinary, full of "ums" and half-sentences—because that's real life.

The Couples Script

Scenario: Partner A vents about their workday. Partner B practices mirroring instead of fixing.

Partner A: Ugh, today was brutal. My manager dumped a last-minute project on me, and I was already swamped.
Partner B: So it felt like way too much landed on your plate all at once?
Partner A: Exactly. And then when I said I'd need help, she just gave me that look—like I should already know how to juggle it.
Partner B: That must've felt pretty dismissive, like she didn't get how much you were already handling.
Partner A: Yes! Thank you. That's exactly it. I just needed someone to hear that.
Partner B: (pauses, nods) Sounds rough. Would you like me to just listen, or brainstorm with you?
Partner A: Just listen for now. Thanks.

The Coworker Feedback Loop

Scenario: Boss gives vague feedback. Employee listens, mirrors, and clarifies.

Boss: You need to be more proactive.
Employee: Okay, can you tell me a bit more about what "proactive"

looks like to you?

Boss: Well… for example, in meetings, I want you to jump in with your perspective instead of waiting until the end.

Employee: So being proactive, in this case, means speaking up earlier—even if my idea isn't fully polished yet?

Boss: Exactly. I'd like to hear your thoughts as they develop.

Employee: Got it. Thanks for clarifying. I'll try that at tomorrow's meeting.

The Friend in Crisis

Scenario: Friend dumps bad news. Listener stays quiet, then offers one sentence of support.

Friend: (sighs) My car broke down again, and now the mechanic says it's the transmission. I can't afford that. Honestly, I don't even know how I'm going to get to work next week. Everything just keeps piling up.

(Listener stays quiet, letting them finish.)

Listener: That sounds really overwhelming—you're carrying so much right now.

Friend: Yeah. (sighs) Just saying it out loud helps a little.

Listener: I'm here. You don't have to figure this all out alone.

Notice how in each case the "listener" doesn't swoop in with solutions. Instead, they mirror, clarify, or just hold space—and the conversation actually deepens.

***

Listening isn't something you "achieve"—it's something you practice. These labs are less about grading yourself and more about experimenting with new ways to tune in. You'll surprise yourself with how quickly the little things (a pause, a mirror, a boundary) shift the entire tone of your relationships.

Chapter 14

Celebrity Case Studies (Good, Bad, Ugly)

Sometimes studying mastery requires seeing greatness in action—and then watching what happens when it falls apart. Here, we'll examine great listening, bad listening, and one particularly egregious failure that hurts because it came from someone who was supposed to help.

The Good: Masterclass Listening

Oprah with Meghan and Harry

In one of her most seismic interviews, Oprah didn't just host a conversation—she built a sanctuary. She asked gentle but potent questions, such as, *"Were you silent, or were you silenced?"* and then paused. Not to fill the void, but to let it sink in. (You could feel those pauses on your sofa.) The couple didn't just talk—they breathed truth into silence, and Oprah listened breathlessly. This is rigorous empathy, where silence isn't awkward—it's an invitation to deeper reality.[21]

Oprah's Method—Why It Works

- Reflective Listening & Follow-ups: She's known for repeating phrases like "That sounds tough for you to deal with as a kid…"—not as mimicry but as emotional anchor points.[22]

- Command of Silence: When she pauses, guests stumble past the point of comfort and into clarity. "Silence feels awkward," says interviewer Grace Ueng, but Oprah leans into it.

Terry Gross on Fresh Air

Terry Gross isn't Oprah with candles—she's Oprah in brain surgery scrubs. One Fresh Air producer described her approach this way: *"She homed in on the most interesting parts, distilled them, and let them breathe."* She asks intimate questions few expect: not what you do, but *why* and *how*. Her sincerity and preparation transform interviews into emotional excavation sites.[23]

Her deep curiosity is unspoken before the mic drops—she's already scooting closer, ready for truth.

---

[21] • Oprah interviewed Meghan & Harry; empathy and structure of question. Press Club Institute+6LinkedIn+6Wikipedia+6The New Yorker+1

[22] • Oprah's reflective listening, silence, empathy. Business InsiderLinkedInJane Adshead Grant

[23] • Terry Gross' technique: deep research, curiosity, emotional excavation. Reddit+7Audible.com+7Wikipedia+7

The Bad: Listening Fails That Burned the Mic

Even in celebrity interviews, not every question lands. I've seen hosts steamroll vulnerability with hot takes, sponsors, or bland pivots. The energy drains out. You feel dismissed. These examples aren't usually malicious—but they're distractions. Because the moment wasn't protected, it died. That's what happens when curiosity gets replaced with clicks.

Even famous interviews can go sideways when listening takes a back seat. Here are three emblematic failures, each with a lesson in what *not* to do:

Natalie Bennett's Housing Interview (With Nick Ferrari)

What went wrong: During a 2015 radio segment, interviewer Nick Ferrari pressed Green Party leader Natalie Bennett on affordable housing. She seemed ill-prepared to answer specifics, fumbling through claims rather than owning her message. Ferrari sensed her uncertainty and kept pressing without offering clarity or helping guide the conversation—making her sound flustered, unfocused, and even untrustworthy.[24]

Why the listening failed: The interviewer wasn't listening for understanding—he was hunting for a mistake. Closing down someone's voice when they're struggling doesn't reveal truth; it destroys credibility.

---

[24] Natalie Bennett interview: The Gong Blog: Five Examples of Media Interviews Gone Wrong en.wikipedia.orghodgespart.com+1

Lesson: If your conversation partner is stumbling, lean in with a clarifying question, not a spotlight—"What does affordable look like to you?" not "That's not a plan."

Madonna on Letterman (1994)

What happened: Madonna's 1994 appearance on *The Late Show* with David Letterman spiralled into shock theatre. Profanity flew; she refused to leave the set, offered her underwear for the host to smell—this was theatre masquerading as an interview.[25]

Why it failed in listening: Neither side listened. Madonna wasn't actually engaging—she was performing. And Letterman hadn't built enough safety or curiosity to rein in (or redirect) the chaos. The moment wasn't used to connect—it was used to shock.

Lesson: In emotionally volatile settings, structure and boundaries matter. Without them, listening turns into a spectacle.

NPR Guest Walks Out on *Fresh Air*

Terry Gross has had to face walkouts from guests like Bill O'Reilly and Gene Simmons mid-interview. Often, her sincerity, intensity, or willingness to probe uncomfortable areas prompts people to back away.[26]

Why it failed listening: Those guests couldn't handle being deeply heard—or being asked emotionally charged questions. They ran from tension instead of leaning into the discomfort.

---

[25] Madonna on Letterman: Madonna on the Late Show with David Letterman in 1994 en.wikipedia.org

[26] Terry Gross walkouts: Wikipedia summary of Terry Gross' career and guest challenges en.wikipedia.org

Lesson: Listening is not always easy or neat. It can push people past their comfort zones. Which is fine—just don't feign neutrality when you're actively challenging them.

Why These Examples Matter

- They show that not listening is active, not passive—and it damages.

- They reveal that failing to listen with curiosity often leads the speaker to either curl up or explode.

- They remind us that cultivating listening isn't a soft skill— it's a responsibility.

Beyond the Spotlight: Leaders Who Listen

It's not just talk-show hosts or celebrities who rise and fall on their listening skills. Some of the most effective leaders in politics, sports, and business have used listening as their superpower.

1. **Politics: Barack Obama's Pauses**
   - Obama was famous — sometimes mocked — for his long pauses before answering. But that pause wasn't hesitation; it was signal. It told the listener: *I heard you, I'm considering, and my response is deliberate.* Contrast that with Donald Trump's debate style — constant interruptions, dominance plays, and flood-the-zone chatter. One projects thoughtfulness; the other bulldozes. Guess which approach builds more trust?[27]

2. **Sports: Phil Jackson's Zen Silence**

---

[27] e.g., Lim, E. T. (2008). *The Anti-Intellectual Presidency: The Decline of Presidential Rhetoric from George Washington to George W. Bush.* Oxford University Press

- As head coach of the Chicago Bulls and L.A. Lakers, Jackson managed titans like Michael Jordan, Kobe Bryant, and Shaquille O'Neal. His secret? Silence. Jackson used presence — long pauses, few words — to ground his players. Instead of shouting over egos, he created space for them to hear themselves. Players later said they felt more respected because he didn't crowd their voices.[28]

1. **Business: Satya Nadella's Listening Reset**

- When Nadella took over as CEO of Microsoft, the company had a reputation for arrogance and internal turf wars. Nadella flipped the script. Instead of lecturing, he started with listening. He asked teams about their struggles, validated concerns, and then steered strategy. That shift toward empathy wasn't just soft skills — it helped rebuild Microsoft's culture and made it one of the most valuable companies on the planet.[29]

Whether it's a debate stage, a locker room, or a boardroom, the leaders who leave a mark aren't always the loudest — they're the ones who shut up long enough for others to be heard.

The Ugly: A Therapist Who Didn't Listen

Now, for a moment, that hits home.

My son—let's call him Robert—was eight. He had written a terrifyingly detailed "old suicide plan." We spent the day at the

---

[28] *Sacred Hoops: Spiritual Lessons of a Hardwood Warrior* (1995) and later in *Eleven Rings: The Soul of Success* (2013

[29] *Hit Refresh: The Quest to Rediscover Microsoft's Soul and Imagine a Better Future for Everyone* (2017)

doctor's office. They were gentle, precise, and left with a plan that felt hopeful. Robert had art therapy that evening, and I asked if he wanted to skip. His answer: "No. I like art. But I don't want to talk about the letter today."

I called his therapist to explain; this was important to him. Robert, for the first time, came to therapy with his own questions prepared.

The therapist placated him, "Yes, I see," over and over, with the emotional investment of a voicemail. Then she steamrolled him, saying she had a "moral obligation" to discuss the letter. My son froze. For the rest of the session, he painted black—page after page. And then said: Never again.

That was the moment she broke trust—and not just with him, but with me as a mother trying to give Robert the tools to navigate huge hurdles.

> She had presence—but no empathy.
> She checked boxes—but didn't check in.
> She listened—but didn't hear.

We never returned to art therapy. It took Robert a while to feel comfortable again with a therapist.

Why These Stories Matter

- Oprah and Terry Gross teach us that listening means creating space—emotionally and structurally—for truth to emerge.

- My therapist anecdote warns that listening without respect can crack open wounds instead of healing them.

***

Whether it's a global icon or someone we ought to trust implicitly, listening well (and poorly) isn't about technique alone— it's about presence, purpose, and human alignment. If Oprah's silence can open vaults, and my therapist's words can shut them, what does that say about the weight we carry in our own listening choices?

> **Reflection Prompt:**
> Quick jot → Which public figure do you think models good listening? Who's terrible?
>
> Medium reflection → Write about one interview or public moment that stuck with you. Why?
>
> Deep journaling → Journal how you'd like to be remembered as a listener in your own "public moments.

Epilogue

We've covered a lot of ground together — the science, the humour, the awkward silences, the role-plays, and the real-life wins and fails. But underneath all of it is something simple and deeply human: the fact that listening changes people. It changes conversations, relationships, and entire communities.

Think back to the moments we've explored: the couple who turned a fight into a breakthrough simply because one person stopped defending and started reflecting. The leader who finally heard the quietest voice in the room and discovered the idea that saved the project. Or maybe you've already started to notice it yourself — that when you put your phone down, make eye contact, and let someone finish a thought, they soften. Their story deepens. They start to trust you with the parts of themselves they usually keep hidden.

Listening may not cure cancer or end war overnight. But it does something just as revolutionary: it restores connection in a fractured world. It creates pockets of safety where truth can breathe. It reminds us that beneath the noise, we're all just humans trying to be heard.

Changing the world starts with listening outward — to partners, colleagues, strangers, and the people you usually tune out. But sustaining it starts with listening inward. The better you hear yourself, the steadier you'll be when the noise of the world tries to pull you under.

So here's my final challenge to you: take on the **7-Day Listening Reboot.**

- **Day 1: No Interruptions.** Bite your tongue. Let people finish.

- **Day 2: Validation Only.** No advice, no fixes — just "I hear you."

- **Day 3: Mirroring.** Paraphrase back what you heard. Watch people light up.

- **Day 4: Curiosity.** Ask three follow-up questions in every conversation.

- **Day 5: Boundary Practice.** Listen, then say no kindly and clearly.

- **Day 6: Silent Support.** Sit with someone without trying to fill the air.

- **Day 7: Gratitude.** Share with someone what you've learned from listening to them.

Seven days. That's it. A week of listening on purpose. And if you do it, you'll never go back. Once you experience how radically different conversations feel when you show up as a true listener, you'll realize this isn't a trick — it's who you've been capable of being all along.

The world doesn't need more people talking louder. It needs more people to listen more deeply.

So go out there. Be the one who listens when no one else will.

Because in a world addicted to noise, the most radical thing you can do is shut the f*ck up — and listen.

Thank You for Reading

Thank you for joining me on this journey—I'm so grateful for your time and support! Your feedback means a lot to me, and hearing from readers is one of the best parts of being an author. If you enjoyed the book, I'd love it if you could take a moment to share your thoughts in a review on Amazon. Your reviews help other readers discover my work, and I appreciate every word.

If you'd like to reach out directly, feel free to contact me at Kelsey.Pearce.Grit@gmail.com. I'd be delighted to hear from you!

With heartfelt thanks,

Kelsey

Other Works by Kelsey Pearce:

Resiliency and Gratitude Series:

Grateful Grit: Building Resilience Through Gratitude ISBN 978-1738290529

Happiness for the Senses: Mindful Sensory Experience: Taste, Touch, Sight, Smell, Sound ISBN 978-1738290505

www.ingramcontent.com/pod-product-compliance
Lightning Source LLC
Chambersburg PA
CBHW072025040426
42447CB00009B/1729